Introduction
1. SENTIENT PORTALS
2. SOMETHING BIG is COMING
3. CULPABILITY is not MORALITY
4. PHYSICS of CREATING
5. WE need to STEP UP and take ACTION
6. CONTRACTS with ALIEN GREYS
7. LIGHT, DARK and LIGHT AGAIN
8. WINDOWS of OPPORTUNITY
9. PLANETS are HALLOW
10. LEADERLESS MOVEMENT into LIGHT

11. FEELING WHEN the dark ones SIPHON

Introduction

Different vibrations have different truths. Portals or parallel universes or time gates, doors or different realities are entrances into other frequencies or vibrations. Portals are growing in size, number and dimension resonating to the high 4th and 5th dimension. Portals are pure awareness and held open with your awareness. There is now enough compassion on earth to balance the fear emanating from the dark ones.

The ascension in process is GALACTIC and PLANETARY. This ascension is also HUMAN ASCENSION when the INDIVIDUAL chooses it. The individuals on and in the earth can be divided into three different groups. One group is moving to the 5th dimension, beyond the fear and into unconditional love. The second group stays in 4th dimension until they are emotionally aligned closer to universal law. And the third group has chosen to experience more drama and battle between light and dark, someplace else.

Nature is acting like it is spring in January 2012 because there is so much energy heating up everything on earth. Step-by-step it's happening. Below is a partial list of dates and markers to indicate light and compassion is here to stay. Unity and peace on earth will be achieved WITHOUT leadership or a hierarchy. Force and fear of the biggest bully is a dark truth. The dark is rapidly losing their ability to scare us. The energy that encourages dissent, distrust and disagreement, is dissipating.

By divine intervention and the good will and wisdom of the Galactic society they are rendering the dark and Illuminati harmless so we can take back control of our planet giving us the responsibility to act on our choices. The individual that learns for them self is being spiritual and following divine will. All paths to higher vibrations are traveled from within the individual.

SOME MARKERS of our INCREASE in VIBRATION

1914 to 2100 Gaia started her winds of change for her 6th ascension.

1945 humanity made a course correction from a de- sire to follow the leader to trust and FOLLOWING your own heart.

SOUL GROUP INCARNATIONS happen when a higher vibrating group wants to assist a lower vibrating group to increase the light they can carry. The Indigo children arrive en masse in the middle 1970s to middle 1990s. Crystals 1980s to 2000, Rainbow 1990s thru 2010 and the Inte- grated child is starting to arrive.

1987 to 2012 was the 25-year Millennium Shift.
August 16-17, 1987 HARMONIC CONVERGENCE marked the first time since the deluge of Atlantis that earth carried equal amounts of light and dark energy and a vibration of spiritual neutrality. Human consciousness as a group was given permission to evolve out of and release duality. Reject our karmic set up and the call to oneness was sounded.
May 1998 the earth entrained with the photon belt and the first of its twelve gigantic homogenizing vortexes of light HIGHLY magnetically charged. These frequencies are to rebalance all that enter. It takes 2,000 years to pass through all the vortexes.

2001 the earth, many humans, cetaceans, animals, plants and the mineral kingdom moved to the 4th dimension.

2007 to speed up the ascension process, our soul aspects grouped many experiences having the same issue in a BUNDLE for us to own and heal consciously all at one time.

2009 has been the first year that the entire population is at a vibration that can communicate with pictures or telepathically.

December 2009 higher vibrations have interfered with our ability to deny.

March 2011 the lower 4th dimension stopped exist- ing with all the lost gray souls it held locked in dark pat- terns of victimhood and the predator cycles. These entities have been relocated and are gone from the earth.

May 21, 2011 souls or any entity or fetus with more DARK than light are unable to incarnate on earth. Dark ancestors can no longer incarnate into biology. Parents with less than 36% light will have soulless infants.

November 11, 2011 we moved from human law into UNIVERSAL LAW. "Give and receive only compassion" and now we are 100% responsible for all we create in our life. The dark ones are no longer running things but many are still in denial and throwing tantrums.

November 16, 2011 the light galactic community put a stop to the broadcasting of the ELF, Extremely Low Frequency waves at 50–80 Hz put out by the illuminati or the elite few that actually have run our world and us. Their underground network of bases and their main transit facilities are out of business.

December 10-12, 2011 was the tipping point on earth from dark to light. Dark was displaced from their state of stable equilibrium into unbalance and chaos. Our collective consciousness is not trapped any longer in fear.

January 1, 2012 marks the separation of the dark or light group on earth you are entrained with. 46% are moving to greater darkness and relocation as they loose their biology. Dark is being relocated and refused entry onto the earth and that increases the amount of light for those that stay and transition.

In 2010, 26% of earth's population carried more light than dark.

In 2012, 54% of those on earth are carrying more light than dark.

2010 the Milky Way populations broke down into 70% human, 25% reptilian and 5% of other. 2012 the Milky Way populations is 79% human, 14% reptilian and 8% others.

January 26, 2012 a portal was opened for all the pieces, aspects and demons left on earth of those souls that have been relocated to join their creators. The energy left in these demons and dark tools were undermining the LIGHT illuminati members restructuring the world finance and policies.

February 2012 Dark ones consume more than they create. They know what they need to do spiritually, but DON'T WANT TO, so there are immediate natural karmic consequences. Dark is being exposed and losing their jobs. February 5, 2012 "NFL half time" was a last ditch ef- fort by the illuminati to create WW III by harnessing the sexual energy generated during the "satanic ritual" or half time and redirecting that energy to intensify the conflict with Iran and Israel. Six days later Whitney Houston was another ritual sacrifice for the Satanists to collect energy and money.

February 27, 2012 a portal of energy was opened to support humans in their love, acceptance and nurturing of the self.

November 2012 all of the 4th dimension will have dissipated or been relocated. The light Gaia carries will need to be consistently at 94% to invite the galactic community in.

HOLDING THEIR LIGHT or SERVICE to OTHERS, many spiritual writers say the plant, animal, elementals and mineral kingdoms volunteered to come to earth to help humans "hold their light" or you will hear that Sam holds light for Kelly. That is another way to say lighter groups and individuals have allowed darker groups or individuals to siphon their light. This makes the lighter person go darker and the darker one a bit lighter. That way the darker one FELT loved, fed or nurtured. As a planet, individual humans and sentient beings we are releasing that dark truth and moving to a higher truth. Each individual needs to hold his or her own light and THEIR compassion for the self.

Compassion for YOU needs to be first. Then the com- passion you give others is pure. When you don't care for you first what you give is tainted with your neediness, darkness, negativity or unconsciousness. Caretaking and service to others first has been glamorized especially by religions to keep us in line and working hard for the top of the pyramid or our needy parent, spouse or boss. Caretaking, enabling and service to others first is a way to blackmail others into valuing you because you have been taught NOT to value yourself. When you sacrifice for another that is very tainted and poisonous to the one you gift your sacrifice too. The individual chooses the speed and direction they want to align with GIVE and receive only COMPASSION.

□□

1. SENTIENT PORTALS

Sentient is the ability to feel and perceive, to think and be aware. Portals exist beyond time and space and live in the now moment. Besides being sentient portals are composed of many different elements that include mathematics, physical matter and our mental beliefs. They take awareness, willingness and skill to navigate. As we move deeper and deeper into the photon belt and higher vibrations we are gradually recalibrating our personal and planetary reality higher and higher in vibration. More and more portals become available to us in higher vibrations. Raising your personal vibration FIRST raises the planetary vibration collectively or the collective vibration can raise your vibration.

All the sentient beings on and in earth are in a continuous pattern of releasing the old dark ways of survival and are using and integrating new light ways of operating. We stop seeing the self as a victim or predator or winner or loser. We realize we are the creators of our own reality. Our old thought patterns of fear and complaining were based on thinking that hard work and suffering were noble when in reality we were serving a master and giving our power away. We are replacing those beliefs with the peace and joy of living in harmony and agreement.

Generation after generation humanity taught and reinforced fear, denial and ignorance. Transporting yourself in something other than a vehicle or airplane can be problematic for us mentally as it goes against our programming of what is possible. If you think something is possible you can adjust your awareness to the frequency or vibration that a particular portal occurs in naturally. When your vibration is high enough to perceive the portal you can open it. Your perception can be visual or you may feel or hear a portal or have a knowingness that it exists. Initially your perception of portals will be through your imagination until you release your limited beliefs about sentient portals living in the now moment.

When you can resonate beyond time and space you will not leave your biology. There is no need to leave or come back because you are everywhere. To enter or use a portal you must release your ATTACHMENT to the physical and to any fears you may be clinging to consciously or unconsciously. Know you exist and are everywhere. You expand your consciousness to become the portal or corridor. Then you compress your essence or awareness into a tiny bit of pure consciousness or light. The distance between Light and Light is zero. Light is compassion or a pulsing portal of light. Portals are live entities. They are an element of your life and yet independent of you.

Entering a portal collapses time and space into the now moment. Our portal will close when our thoughts go dark or our vibration slows too much to stay in the vibration of the portal. Your journey in a portal is fueled by your imagination and 5th dimension thought or compassion. This is a change in your frequency not your location. Within the portal or corridor you are still within your SELF. Eventually you can move from opening a portal to becoming the portal you opened. Then you are ready to move through the portal as it moves through you. Are you still with me?

Our THOUGHT PATTERNS travel in waves and have a certain frequency. The micro-crystals in the pineal gland pick up, store and transmit information the way computer software does. Our stored habits of fearfulness thought patterns create a compulsion in us to keep doing what we have done in the past. To override your darker patterns you need to be conscious about what you do think. Fearful thought patterns carry a low vibration calibrating the pineal portal to lower light along with the human. As your vibration increases old habits and memories of fear and darkness are pushed to your awareness to be released. Most of this fear is ancient but attaches itself to anything similar going on in your life in present time. Suppression, denial and trying to put off your awareness will attach you to a lower vibration. Being sentient, feeling and aware means you are connected to you first and then to others on the same vibration. You know when you have created psychic or physical pain for you. When you have decided to stop causing that pain or any suffering for you.

The round time loop or cycle of ancient history during the dark times of Atlantis is attaching to us as a group in present time to allow us the opportunity to rewrite those events and move to greater light. Instead of having com- passion for the self, DARK ones resorted to control and force or tormenting and experimentation on others. Their experiments created great pain, suffering and fear that be- came part of the COLLECTIVE and PLANETARY awareness and consciousness. The earth vibration fell from high forth dimension to the lowest fourth dimension on into the third dimension of physicality.

That was so low the holographic matrix was beginning to degrade. Gaia sent out a call for assistance from the higher dimensions to help raise our vibration. Volunteers entered our holographic to mend the matrix and were successful in keeping the matrix together but the vibration of 3rd dimension became the permanent resonance of earth for the next 10,000 years. The fear lowered the matrix from that of playfulness and creativity of the higher 4th dimension into the extreme polarities of light and dark, male and female. We polarized ourselves into the dark little human forcing others being compassionate creators infrequently.

Portals, planets, solar systems, galaxies and humans are sentient. There is a joint illusion of time and space about the earth's rotation around the holographic galaxy and that includes the photon belt showing up every 10,000 years to balance out the vibrations on earth. We entered the first of the twelve vortexes of the photon belt in 1998. The gigantic vortexes are magnetic "light charged frequencies" to homogenize and rebalance all that enter. Waves of light are being released from the sun onto earth at various inter- vals particularly at the time of the EQUINOX in March and September and SOLSTICES in June and December each year. As it intensifies deeper spiritual cleansing and balancing will adjust our consciousness and awareness or we will be relocated and recalibrated. The more imbalanced we are the more disruption and internal conflict we will have during the next 2,000 years of rebalancing.

The Kali Yuga is the 2,000-year cycle furthest from the last trip or during Atlantis and the last 2,000 years through the Photon Belt. By the Kali Yuga or final cycle out of the photon belt or at the end of ten thousand years there is re- entry into the photon belt and re-start of the holographic projection of form in the lower dimensions and another two thousand years of rebalance. It will take earth 2,000 years to pass completely through the 12 vortexes. During this process SEPARATION between the dimensions become thinner and thinner or goes away completely. Once we leave the Photon Belt, we go through five two-thou- sand-year cycles.

Logging-out of this hologram is not dying or loss of your biology. To log-out of this vibration you need to be compassionate with you and in aligning with universal law. During the darker times of Atlantis many sentient beings chose to log-out of the hologram or moved to inside the hollow earth before the last trip through the photon belt. Many from Atlantis chose to remain in the hologram to re- pair the damage they created with their dark thought and nuclear weapons. Gaia sent out a distress call and many light Beings answered her call and agreed to continue assisting our matrix through the next 10,000-year cycle before the reentry into the photon belt, which stared in 1998.

□□

KINDS of PORTALS

PARALLEL UNIVERSES or PORTALS or time gates, doors or different realities are entrances into other frequencies or vibrations. Portals have always existed on earth but are growing in size, number and dimension with the higher vibrations. Portals are created mathematically with the algorithms of interwoven energy. There are countless numbers of portals to access when you log out of 3rd and the lower 4th dimensions and our matrix and then log into higher dimensions. We are all thought without our biology or the duality matrix.

The VORTEX is a mass of whirling fluid or air, a whirl- pool or whirlwind. The seen part of the vortex is the spiral- ing arms of energy that extend out from the unseen source of energy that generates the vortex similar to those of our galaxy. The atmospheric phenomenon of a tornado or dust devil forms a helix, column, or spiral or vortices of energy. Turbulent energy flows can make multiple vortices. When a vortex has a lot of light that many have now they can turn into portals and can move.

Vortexes go up and have an airy smell. In the Northern Hemisphere they rotate clockwise in the Southern Hemisphere they rotate counter-clockwise. A vortex is also known as a wormhole, portal or corridor. Portals are vortexes that exist in places where the transmutation of 3rd dimension into the 4th dimension has been completed. Gaia resonates to different dimensions in different areas at different times depending on the vibration of various life forms in that spot on her or in her.

UNIVERSAL or CELESTIAL PORTALS are generally inter-planetary or inter-galactic portals. Some of these universal portals are only open during certain lunar and stellar alignments and cycles. For example full moons or eclipses.

The BLACK HOLE is a region in space having a gravitational field so intense that no matter or radiation can escape. In quantum physics black holes are energy vortexes of immense size and power. Black holes draw approaching energy or matter toward its core located in another dimension. WHITE HOLES do exist and are twinned with black holes. They are cosmic electrical forces with a strong crystalline influence. Everything is electrically charged in the universe or cosmos.

The WORMHOLE is two black holes stuck together end to end bonded to the other and a method of traveling in one direction. You have to manipulate your consciousness to move forward to a point. And find another way back. Wormholes open an energetic shortcut from point A to point B in the SAME reality. The technology can pin point your bedroom and take you while putting a dampening on others in the house so they don't notice your absence.

A CORRIDOR is a portal that is not connected to land it is located in outer space. A corridor is a distribution center to be passed through to get from place to place in the universe. There are thousands of corridors around us with all different purposes. The Arcturian Corridor is close to earth because we are ascending into higher dimensions. The Arcturian Corridor can have as many corridors in as many places as are needed OR it can be one corridor with openings to many different realities accommodating all the creators. Going into this corridor is similar to going into the great void because it is in-between all-possible realities and a gateway to every reality.

The Arcturian Corridor is a portal for every person, animal, plant and entity on or in the body of Gaia. It is a way station for nonphysical consciousness to become accustomed to physicality. Entering the corridor allows your soul to be transported to another incarnation or planet or move out to other solar systems and dimensions. We enter the corridor during sleep or in a meditative state to slowly evolve, release pockets of density and raise our vibration. Clearing unconscious and conscious beliefs of limitation and feelings of separation.

On September 9th, 2002 an inner portal in the Arcturian Corridor was intensified and opened for all 3rd and 4th dimension people, planets and realities to enter to start the process of increasing their vibration. This portal has been in place for eons but is only opened during dimensional alignments. Inside the corridor is harmonic resonance and colors to activate genetic restructuring and higher vibration skills like the ability to travel and communicate with all entities in the universe.

STAR GATES are constructed technologically and do not occur NATURALLY as vortexes do. The star gate is a circular object constructed of the elements FOUND of the world the star gate is placed on for example a pyramid. There were many star gates constructed on earth to connect us to many other worlds of a SIMILAR vibration to the one we have. They are gateways for inter planetary and inter galactic travel for those not limited by this illusion.

Our leaders, secret societies and the military discovered star gates and other similar devices long ago. Unfortunately they used them for negative and selfish reasons causing more damage to Gaia and humanity. The little human is interested in seeking power-over others. All energy travels in circles so when your intention is negative it will return to the sender to receive what was sent.

Generally the awareness of those that entered a star gate got confused. They believed they traveled far through space when in reality they entered one of the many parallel worlds or the lower 4th dimension or worlds of dark vibrations. Now most Star gates have been disassembled.

TEMPORARY PORTALS found on earth. There are earthly portals opened by our compassion for Gaia and portals in space opened by our compassion for our soul. These portals are always available beyond limited 3rd dimensional perceptions.

The crop circle is a temporary and inter-dimension-al portal. An entity from another planet or galaxy is not bound by earth's collective consciousness or limitations. They can use the temporary crop circles as an inter-dimensional portal and can teleport themselves to their destination with the power of their expanded thoughts, feelings, beliefs and expectations.

There are ancient BREATHING PORTALS on Gaia one is located in Sedona Arizona. This is a physical portal. The portal is always open and not controlled by dark or light. There are portals CREATED by the population as in Phoenix Arizona. The more a created portal is used the longer it will stay open. Dark can highjack a light portal but then the portal may not stay open.

EXPECTATION PORTALS are opened solely by the expectation or feelings of the entity close to a possible portal. There are many entities or life forms with great power that visit and live on our planet we most likely are not aware of. They easily perceive portals and can open them with their expectation because their consciousness resonates or vibrates high enough to recognize and open the portal. If you can perceive it you can open it. Perception includes seeing, feeling, hearing or your knowingness. We start by perceiving portals in our imagination.

For example you can help a confused entity, soul or animal to greater light and understanding by opening a portal in your imagination of greater light for them to go through if they would like that. Invite anyone else that may be around to move to the portal of greater light, compassion and understanding. ef

□□

PERSONAL PORTALS

The act of asking aloud for assistance opens a portal of two-way communication between you and your soul aspect. The reptilians changed human geneticists by put-ting us in so much fear we switched off our access to the invisible realm. It is time to reclaim access.

Portals are live entities or sentient beings therefore they will have their own vibration and purpose. When you can match your vibration to perceive the portal you can open it. Your perception can be visual or you may feel or hear a portal or you have a knowingness that it exists and some people only experience portals while asleep. Initially your perception of your personal portals will be through your imagination until you release your limited beliefs. Newcomers to the Arcturian Corridor enter through a smaller portal that instantly monitors their level of fears. When there is any fear helpers come to assist new arrivals to calm their fears and calibrate their vibration. Entering a portal collapses your concept of time and space into the now moment suspending any limited or linear beliefs of what is possible or true.

Instead of visualizing you as a human consider seeing you as light or an individual photon. LIGHT is an energy that crosses all dimensions simultaneously. Light is everywhere all the time. Compress your essence or awareness into a tiny bit of pure consciousness or light. Then expand your essence to become the portal or corridor. You can easily move to large or small. As the spin of the portal increases the portal opens. Eventually you go from opening a portal to becoming the portal you opened. Travel in the portal is different than using a car, it constantly changes sizes and spins. As you move through the portal it moves through you. There is a melding or overlap to share consciousness. Portals will close when your thoughts go dark or when they move into lower vibration. When you get fearful or in doubt portals will close. In higher vibrations there is nothing to fear in low vibrations or dealing with dark individuals fear protects you and is needed to survive.

When we are in Alpha brainwaves and beyond we become a portal of light or vortex for higher frequency energies to enter our bodies. Our BIOLOGY is the personal portal into this matrix or holographic experience of 3rd and 4th dimension and duality. Our RNA/DNA is a portal around us. Our fears have kept our personal portals closed. When you vibrate high enough to keep your personal portals open things change in you. Your perceptions increase permanently. Your brainwaves and your state of awareness move from Beta to Alpha, Theta, and even Delta. Your biology will need to release areas of density, tension or weakness. In the process you will suffer varying physical symptom.

Our RNA/DNA is a portal around us. The human bi- ology is a map or blueprint that could replicate itself into perfection before we were tampered with physically and genetically. Emotionally, spiritually and physically we have added stress and fear to our bodies and that deteriorates its precise mechanisms. We have codes embedded in our DNA strands inside and outside the biology that work together as one unit. Our DNA controls this entire illusion or matrix. The DNA codes receive information and instructions magnetically and electronically to relay information to our cells. DNA is not specific it is identical all over the body. DNA communicates with itself and knows what is happening in every part of our four bodies. DNA can be programmed with words, frequencies, sounds, light or all three.

The default belief of survival is fight or flight that our reptilian brain functions with. The portal to duality gradual- ly became a prison for our consciousness. Our DNA is spiritually intelligent when the human vibrates high enough to allow it to work. A 3rd strand of RNA/DNA is being added to those spiritually evolving and shows up in the new soul groups of children.

Our THYMUS gland and the heart chakra allows light in from higher vibrations to heal our wounds, traumas, trans- mutes darkness and fear into light and rules our immune system. The heart chakra rules the lungs. The best way to calm your entire body is through your breath. A long slow deep inhale opens the heart's portal and serves as our grounding point. Breathe in through the opened third eye to pull in universal energy with serotonin to calm you and melatonin to enlighten you. Breathe out through your high heart or thymus to expand your acceptance of unconditional love and emanate compassion through out your en- tire body. The more you become a conscious breather the more you activate the thymus and your immune system. When the pineal gland gets excess electrical stimulation the thymus breathing brings calm and peace.

Our THIRD EYE or the pineal gland and the crown chakra in the center of our brain behind the pituitary gland of your brow chakra serve as our control tower portal. This portal opens the POINTS of INTEGRATION of the horizontal, 3rd dimension and higher dimensional realities allowing the cosmic flow into the thymus gland portal. This opening occurs by combining the physical energies of your first through sixth chakras with the pineal gland of the crown chakra. When the third eye is opened the pineal portal be- gins its return to full activation. The opened third eye is a portal of renovation to higher IQs and reconnection of the two halves of our brain.

When you first open your pineal portal you may receive auditory messages. To convert auditory messages to the LANGUAGE of LIGHT you need to raise your frequency by forty octaves. As the little human surrenders to their soul aspect and universal law their frequency rises be- cause the universal law of entrainment goes into effect to raise the resonance of the lower vibration. The language of light is a series of sounds, symbols and colors and encoded into our DNA as we stay balanced and compassionate our DNA releases more information for us. In 2012 our brains will be able to absorb at least two more octaves of light waves through our pineal gland.

The pineal portal is filled with liquid light and micro- crystals of calcite. CALCITE CRYSTALS were formed in our brains and PINEAL gland about 60 years ago and have been lying dormant waiting to be activated. The pineal portal has two-way communication. The crystals can be focused to receive electromagnetic frequencies like the old quartz radio did. We can communicate with each other through these electromagnetic frequencies or radio waves that have always run through us. Crystals are living holders of information. Crystal or silicon and carbon based structures are only a few molecules away from each other on the PERIODIC TABLE. All life is turning crystalline even viruses and bacteria. Transmutation of lower vibrations into higher vibrations may be sensed in your Crown as a tingling or slight itch at the top of your head. Repetitive tasks may start to bore you or cause fatigue because part of your awareness is bi and tri locating.

Sleep cycles may change, circadian cycles are shifting due to the constant stimulation of your pineal gland. Dreams are move vivid and illumined than before. Ongoing opening of our Third Eye may give sinus headaches, dizziness, colds, postnasal drip, vision problems or difficulty with concentration. Opening of your Third Eye increases your telepathy, empathy, intuition, clairvoyance, and clairaudience, clairsentience.

Combine the third eye and high heart portals into one inter-dimensional portal at your THROAT chakra. Humans are basically receivers in a sea of frequencies of light interference patterns. We choose to perceive and create, our reality from the myriad possible realities. The pineal and the pituitary glands work together. The pituitary gland regulates the secretion of hormones for the entire endocrine system. When the pituitary is over stimulated it can temporarily over stimulate the thyroid gland (throat chakra) and the adrenals (root chakra) producing surges of energy and the feeling of being on a high and can produce adrenal stress, depression or anxiety. The individual can experience extreme physical and emotional symptoms as the body seeks to rebalance itself.

Portals are pure awareness and held open with your awareness your frequency not your location. To perceive the portals you must look INSIDE the self as they are accessed from within each person. All paths to higher vibrations are traveled from within the individual that stays centered, receptive, peaceful and aware. Entering a portal can give you the sensation of confusion or dizziness or you may feel a flow or swirl of energy. Sometimes a dot or color gets larger opening up into a portal. Going through a portal can cleanse, rebalance or expand the biology, heart, brain or consciousness. There is a gauzy covering on the opening of portals to prevent lower vibrating things and entities from entering. Closed a portal looks similar to hands clasped in prayer.

The largest and smallest light particle or PHOTON can merge into one portal of any size you like. You perceive the smallest and largest wormhole or portal as a circular flow of light. LIQUID LIGHT is our awareness of the movement of light as it flows, dances or intermingles. The distance light flows is zero for all light. All movement of light is SPIRAL. The smaller spirals appear circular or elliptical because you cannot see the higher dimensional interactions. Nothing is in a straight line.

You can view many different realities at once. Just as we can see many colors at once each color is distinct and yet blends with all the other realities or colors. We are the OBSERVER and PARTICIPANT in each reality. As you feel each you discern the differences. You can expand to embrace each reality within the self or know the many possible options that are available to sample. When we connect to concurrent lifetimes it is through a portal.

□□

2. SOMETHING BIG is COMING

We are transitioning from human law in the matrix with all its corruption, unfairness and miscarriage's of jus- tice to UNIVERSAL or COSMIC LAW. The vibration of this planet and all the people that will remain on it are to be vibrating at 50-60% light and greater steadily getting lighter. The dark limited thinkers will not be running the world any longer. Systematic ways of decreasing the dark ones have been put in place and are slowly and humanely being implemented. The angelic realm has changed the rules of engagement in the energy wars of dark and light on earth. They are now being proactive.

While maintaining freewill for all the LIGHT is acting

1. May 21, 2011 was the marker for souls or any entity or any fetus that is more dark than light. They are no longer allowed to incarnate on earth. No more dark ancestors incarnating into biology or newborns coming into the family. To incarnate on earth now you need to carry more light than dark. As dark souls are dying off or leaving the planet they are not being replaced with other dark souls. For parents with less than 36% light their newborn will not have a soul. The infant will have flat affect and act like "no one is really home" or empty and it will feel like having a doll that eats and poops or having a robot to interact with. This means the caretaker will not be able to torment the infant, steal or harness their FEAR energy for dark purpose. The soulless infant is useless to the illuminati. Soulless children are not expected to survive much past 2020 because of the increasing higher vibrations on Gaia.

2. November 11, 2011 humans and Gaia moved from human law into universal law. Give and receive only com- passion. The dark ones are no longer running our planet but many are still in denial and throwing tantrums. Still causing chaos for many. This begins an era where the dark ones and their truths no longer control humans. Dark systems of law, finance, religion, dysfunctional family members and other various leaders will no longer govern us.

3. November 16, 2011 the light galactic community put a stop to the broadcasting of the ELF, Extremely Low Frequency waves at 50–80 Hz put out by the illuminati or the elite few that actually have run our world and us. It will take time to work them out of the system. The dark broad- casted a constant stream of ELF waves through all our air- ways to prevent us from communication with our self and our own thoughts. Now it will be easier to commune with your essence.

For decades various secret governments have maintained vast networks of underground and underwater bases. The Galactic community has dismantled the bases and the dark has lost thousands of vital personnel including their exotic research scientists and technicians. Those kept underground and enslaved by the Illuminati were also released. When we are willing they will tell us their stories.

4. December 10-12, 2011 was a total lunar eclipse and more portals opening. This was the tipping point from dark to light. Dark was displaced from a state of stable equilibrium into unbalance and chaos. Our collective conscious ness will not be trapped in the low vibration of fear any longer. When the individual and group vibration is at 60% and more our universe is much easier to keep balanced and harmonious.

When you are able to have compassion for you, tormenting or forcing others will not feel good or enjoyable to you. That means you will never start dark thoughts or you will stop dark behavior on your own. The universal laws and principles are derived from fundamental truths found within universal law. Principles are morally correct attitudes or general scientific theorem or law having many special applications.

The Ten Commandments are the Universal / Quanta Laws simplified as "rules" to point out what is a dark or light thought and choice. Those that believe compassion for the self happens externally and not internally will always "covet" or yearn to possess what another one has. When your belief is that only another person can complete you and give you love, you will never allow others their freedom. Those that worship ANY external "authority" give away their energy, power, thinking and frequently their biology and health.

Consider viewing the soldier or warrior from the point of perception of "Give and receive only unconditional love and compassion." They would be going against the universal law of allowing others to follow the path of their choice. How is killing others that have a different belief than yours or saving them from a bully in alignment with give and receive only compassion. They would also be going against the universal principle of HAPPINESS, which is how you feel about WHOM you are, what you do, and what you have created that creates your happiness.

Universal law is not concerned with punishment like human law is. The laws of attraction and entrainment help you recreate over and over again any pain and suffering your thoughts have created for you. To STOP your suffering CHANGE your thoughts. If you can't play nice the universe will move your essence into a reality that will immerse YOU in more of your negative unconsciousness to experience it over and over until you want to experience something nicer or you go black and get reduced to your quantum state and transmuted.

Consider viewing the criminal and all the money, man power, time and effort spent on catching, blaming the right individual and punishing people that commit crimes and atrocities as a result of their abusive childhoods. Why isn't the focus on nurturing a healthy well balance infant and child that would not even consider criminal behavior as a way to express them self. The child or adult with the indigo color vibration senses dishonesty and corruption. They know when they're being lied to, patronized, or manipulated. The child or adult with the crystal vibration have open HEARTS and unguarded compassion they can read your thoughts and feelings. They are forgiving, modest and incredibly telepathic and have healing abilities. The child or adult with rainbow energy is a fearless giver ready to fulfill our needs. As we rise in vibration we carry all these energies and more.

☐☐

FEELING INTENSIFIES as GRIDS FALL

Motive and intent are more important spiritually than the skills humans mastered to survive in the matrix. Many skills mastered for the third to lower 4th dimension are NOT aligned with universal/quantum law. For example competition is out and equality is in. Self sacrifice and caretaking is over and self-love is in. External approval is over and going within gives peace and knowingness.

The time and space grids that form this matrix of duality and contrast are collapsing. Ever increasing higher vibrating energies are flowing into the grids and portals breaking the dark's hold on earth that they have held captive for the past 13 millennia.

Higher frequencies amplify our thoughts and emotions. When you are self-hating and fearful or angry it will become more intense and painful. When you want to retain power and control over others so you can feel safe, no amount of control will calm your fears. Cruelty to you or others will not give you peace and will increase your frustration and physical discomfort. Those living dark truths are closing them self off from the increasing awareness and light earth is getting. When you are compassionate and supportive with the self your soul aspect will help you block dark energy. The universal law of ACTION means the human must ACT first to prove their commitment to the direction they are moving in. Then your soul aspects will line up synchronicities for you in the vibration or level of compassion you attract.

The universal principle of INERTIA is a body at rest re- mains at rest until an equal and opposite reaction happens moving the body at rest into another direction or vibration or reality or dimension. The principle of LEVERAGE is a small amount of energy exerted in present time is used to change the course of future and past events. A change in your awareness NOW will change your future and past experiences. Time and space are combined in round loops of similar events without past or future and is never fixed or linear. In the 4th dimension time is very mutable. 5th dimension and beyond time is only NOW in alternate realities occurring all at once.

The round loops of SIMILAR events in your experiences are bundled together. Similar loops of awareness about the same subject layered on each other like the string theory is layered. Pure awareness in loops on a theme is in operation when we sleep, meditate or create because then we are thought without our biology or the duality matrix affecting us. The law of attraction pulls similar events together and the law of entrainment holds them together for you to see and understand your thinking.

For example all the times you were cruel and insensitive are all bundled together in loops. You feel justified in being cruel because they are STUPID or UGLY or didn't do what you wanted them to do.

Those thoughts would go against the universal laws of AWARENESS and ALLOWING and ATTRACTION. The universal principle of awareness means you NEED to observe the illusion of separation that duality presents and realize how many dark truths you have accepted and adopted or twisted to consider them to be a light truth. Cruelty and in-sensitivity of any kind or for any justification is a dark truth and will keep you attached to darkness.

The universal law of ALLOWING means you releasing your attachment to forcing the world to conform to what you need. That way you would be more comfortable if they catered to your needs.

The universal law of ATTRACTION reflects with clarity and truth the dark or light beliefs you hold and operate with. Conscious or unconsciously your vibration emanates from you attracting more of what you broadcast out. When you broadcast cruelty and judgment that is exactly what you will receive from others. Was that what you wanted?

Another example of loops of awareness bundled together on a

theme is all the times YOU need others to be the way you want them to be. Because it is for "their own good" and you put all your energy into making them PLEASE your version of reality. How has that come back to you?

Pushing your agenda or using force means you are not allowing others to be on their path. Even when their path is dark and self-destructive it needs to be their choice. Earth's reality or matrix is a role-playing game designed to increase discernment and spiritual wisdom about the way dark behaves and the truths the dark hold and live by. Forcing and pushing your agenda is the energy emanating from you. That attracts more of what you broad- casted back to you. Then you will be forced and pushed to help you decide if that is what you truly want. Being at the mercy of a bully or another controlling you is not a nice experience. Nurturing and showing compassion for the self is way to go. Ascension is out of the question when you fail to nurture and be compassionate with you first. How many dark truths are you still holding in your personal reality?

When the earth vibrated lower than it does now your soul aspects were not allowed to rescue you. When you chose to experience life with dark parents they could not pull us out or protect us from that. We had to cope the best we could with the dark experiences that we chose to gain spiritual wisdom from.

The universal law of FREEWILL is divine will granting each entity the right to direct and pursue his or her existence so long as he or she does not violate the same right of others to live as they wish. A right that excludes the rights of others is NOT DIVINE.

FORGIVING is releasing your judgment of YOU for the things that went on in your experiences. Judgment and condemnation of you creates separation and darkness for you. Forgiving is not a passive act it is a call to ACTION, a time for you to embrace the bigger picture and take your focus off the wound of the little human. Waking up means you NOTICE what is really going on around you and you need to own your part in your creation.

FATIGUE is the result of our 3rd dimensional perceptions and awareness shutting down to make way for a larger operating system to take over. As long as we have two different operating systems working in the same biology we will be fatigued. The places in our biology that we store fear and stress vibrate slower and are sluggish. These pockets of density when released cause physical sensations or discomfort. Choosing to focus on what you enjoy puts you in the reality you wish to resonate with minimizing discomfort. Be as still and calm as possible. Forgive and detach from the illusion we lived in. Failing to own and release your past will deny you living in the present. Redirect your thought. You are what you hold in your thoughts.

We must see and understand how we have been manipulated and moved away from compassion. Globally there will be cooperation, freedom, personal sovereignty, and prosperity for all that want it and are able to have it. The monetary collapse or new wars will not happen. The dark's goal was to reduce the earth's population by nearly 90% with their shots, chemtrails, toxic food, weapons, police brutality but that will not stop the SPIRITUAL awaken- ing that is in process.

□□

EMPTY the OLD and LOAD in the NEW

Early 2011 there was only 3% of the population on earth that operated in PRESENT TIME and is always committed to being compassionate with them self and their biology. They also carry 80% or more light, are joyful, enthusiastic and commune with their soul aspect. By the end of 2011 that number increased to 10% of those on earth and Gaia was at 95% light.

The increased vibrations on earth by the end of 2011 put 10% of the population into zero point energy. That is universal energy at rest or at the lowest level of activity. Your first awareness of zero-point energy may be one of feeling stuck because motion has stopped, become balanced or neutral. From zero-point energy one is ready to create in a state of detachment, joy and compassion. This is releasing the old and putting in a new pattern of spiritual awareness working with your soul aspect.

Others working on more spiritual awareness may have entered the void at the end of the year of 2011. Going into a void, portal or the EMPTY feeling is what we go through when what has been usual and customary for us ends. There is a feeling or sensation of empty aloneness. A void happens after you realize a belief you always operated with is no longer a truth for you. You need to release the old truths before adopting new truths. When your beliefs crumble there is grieving, pain and JOY that can be experienced during this process. Grieve the changes and any lose you might feel.

Cut the cords to relationships no longer serving you. Give back any darkness you have carried for others as a child and especially from family members. Now you can rewrite your concurrent lifetimes. New thoughts will come into your awareness as mental and emotional processing and transmuting go on. Generally voids last a few months or weeks. We go into the void many times this is not a one-time event.

80%ers are those people carrying 80% LIGHT or those vibrating at 80% light or more. They function in present time are enthusiastic and have committed to being com- passionate with them self and their biology. Functioning steadily at 80% light you are vibrating high enough for your soul aspect to enter the space around your biology and "the little human" starts to merge with their soul aspect or surrender to the greater wisdom and alignment with universal law the soul aspect carries.

At 80% light or more you have had your half dark / half light ascension. Your guides, angels, higher self and imaginary friends say good-by one way or another you will notice them leave or you may have a dream about them leaving. You will then go into zero point energy and feel lonely but you are NOT abandoned so have faith. You are not being upgraded. You move into the void and old truths fall away there is a time of calm. It is wise to release and grieve for what you were and what you had experienced. New truths or thought patterns are in the making. You are moving to create with detachment, joy and compassion with greater alignment to universal law.

January 1, 2012 is the marker on earth for the further separation of the entrained groups moving to greater dark- ness and relocation or commitment to moving to greater light and staying on earth. In 2010 only 26% of earth's population carried more light than dark. January 1, 2012 there is 53.84% carrying more light than dark. The percentage of light you carry is based on the spiritual wisdom you have gained in all your incarnations on earth. Your soul aspect will be happy to give you the percentage of light you carry now and or at any other time, just ask! When you are un- able to hear the percentage of light you have from your soul, get a yes or no answer to "Am I more light than dark" YES or NO? Then ask, do I have 60 to 70% light?

The legion of light imposed quarantine or forced isolation of the dark emanating from the earth roughly 12,500 years ago when Atlantis sank and the earth plunged into darkness. We have experienced separation from our soul, frustration, misery and pain to let us know we needed to make different lighter choices. The human with over50% light emanates some grayish light because there is always a hidden agenda and low self esteem with one that is 50 to 60% light. Their light is not pure light. They are able to consciously create some. BUT they do not have compassion for themselves and are frequently caretakers to avoid loving the self. Those with 50 to 60% light will struggle the most as the vibration on earth increases.

Our biology has been a vehicle and learning tool used to have dark experiences with on a planet that emanated dark. With the many little dark choices we have made we gave away our energy (frequently fear energy) to others, leaders and bullies especially found in our families. We stopped thinking for ourselves becoming needy and dependent. As we got increasingly darker we got very attached to what would keep our biology alive. We became physically and emotionally attached to STUFF or people or organizations that we felt could keep the biology safe and satisfied. Most behaviors in the "earth illusion" are about maintaining the biology physically not spiritually.

ONLY when we can carry 60% light most of the time have we started showing compassion for the SELF. You need to be embraced rejected parts of you and integrate them into the whole. When the human consistently carries 65 to 69% light they can tap into the "universal sources of information" them self without an entity as a go between like a guide, angel, ascended master, alien or your higher self. There are no secrets in lighter higher vibrations. Every- one has access to everything.

Carrying 70% light or more an entity or demon can- not posses your biology because you won't let it, you love yourself too much to allow that. You are aware that you have never been a victim and YOU created your victim experiences to increase your understanding of dark truths. The dark presents endless moral dilemmas to mold, develop and shape our moral character. Universal law says all are equal and you are responsible for the self. When you refuse to be responsible for you and what you create you are more dark than light.

☐☐

INFINITE COMPASSION INCREASES in 2012

Compassion will increase because universal energy will have a greater presence on earth in 2012. Universal energy or the cosmic flow or cosmic intelligence or torsion waves is the BASE energy that permeates all life in the universe or cosmos and is infinite compassion with NO agenda or attachments. It has the highest vibration there is and flows a sense of wellbeing, compassion and knowingness through our soul aspects to the human vibrating high enough to sense it. Universal energy feels like you feel when the choir sings. ZERO-POINT energy is the measurement of universal energy at rest. When you are aware of it initially it feels like being stuck because there is no motion but this is the most powerful point a person can attain.

Feeding CORDS will be dissolved for those that carry 60% or more light. DARK soul contracts will have no energy or focus on them. There is a higher percentage of universal energy on earth in 2012 brought by the sun and photon belt and that translates into an over all generalized feeling of wellbeing in lighter humans. People are for- getting why and whom they are angry with in the higher vibrations. Universal energy BLENDS, harmonizes and en- trains all energies. Higher vibrations WAKE UP people put- ting them in present time or get them to THINK and make their personal choices about the direction they want to move in. Universal energy in large amounts makes denial and dissociation increasingly difficult to do.

The universal flow of energy comes to humans through their soul aspect through the opened third eye and is understood by our high heart. We ground the energy from the universe into the earth with our biology and then Gaia amplifies that energy returning it to her surface to expand its radiance over the entire planet.

Anyone can listen or read about morally correct behavior BUT it requires courage, commitment and aware- ness to change your ways and start walking the talk. You NEED to observe the illusion of separation that duality presents. Understand the dark truths to avoid them. Arguing or trying to reason with the dark ones drags you down to their level of awareness. All you can do is walk away from the dark and allow them to continue on their path.

For those that are Illuminati slaves or those gripped by addiction when you are in those states it is because you have had stress and you cope with stress by dissociating and in a dissociated state you are powerless. When a slave or addict is brave enough to stay in present time and BE AWARE of what they do and think, THEN they can decide and act the way they want to.

The illuminati created the various religions on earth with the same satanic themes they brought from Draco. The various religions ALL tell the same stories we find in the bible and other religious texts. The stories are designed to glorify and empower the little human, ego or reptilian. They all carry the same message of follow this deity or be punished or get killed or you will not be saved. All the religions claim to be doing "gods work" by going through the universe dominating and assimilating inferior creatures and making slaves as humans are. With the earth religions we take "natives" or "pagans" land, natural resources and their money and force our "version of god" guilt and control on them.

All the gods in the matrix take your free will and ability to choose and THINK for your self. They keep you focused and fearful with fire and brimstone, or sound and light shows to keep your attention diverted outward. There is little attention paid to what goes on inside you.

PROGRAMMING and ADDICTIONS are stimulus-response or conditioning or associative learning. A significant stimulus evokes a REFLEXIVE response. For example smelling something cooking you like to eat starts the saliva in your mouth flowing. Reading the intention of your predator evokes the reflexive response of dissociation. Having a confrontation about something important to you makes you look for a distraction and you move into some type of robotic action. You get fearful and move into a fantasy world you have total control of. None of that is staying in present time, which is the only time you have the power to create something different for you.

The universal law of ENTRAINMENT REQUIRES all resonances in the same location to fall in sync. Predators and victims do that and that is why they are able to read each other's thoughts and FEELINGS and know what the other plans to do next, like the criminal and law enforcement. Some read the thought, are horrified and they dissociate. As long as they are dissociated they have no control and take on the predators resonance. Entrainment is a locking onto each other, a meeting in the middle or moving to the strongest vibration. This bonding is for dark and or survival reasons UNTIL the point of dissociation. Then the bonding or entrainment is over and you move into programming or addiction.

When we can radiate light and another is open to re- ceive light there is an electrostatic bonding. The two or more become entrained. They feel and are consciously aware of what the other is feeling, thinking and planning to do. This is joyful and affirming.

The universal principle of COMPENSATION is that we receive "like energy" to the energy we emanate in our thought and action. Our reward is as large as you are able to NOTICE and receive graciously. Limitation comes from your refusal to see, own and use the wisdom or clue offered to you. The legion of lights blessings, "gods gifts" or synchronicities need to be allowed in or received by YOU. Religion and darkness have been dismal failures at teach- ing people to love themselves. When you don't love your- self FIRST your ability to love anything or anyone else is drastically reduced to caretaking. With such a low vibration you fail to accept your many gifts and blessings of aware- ness and valuing the self.

When you put your self in the position of becoming a victim you need to rescue yourself. What you have attracted to you needs to be undone by you. The universal law of PERPETUAL TRANSMUTATION of energy is that all humans have the power to change the conditions in their lives. Raising your vibration takes serious spiritual work staying in your biology in present time and focusing your thoughts. We all have the skill set to do that.

All humans have intuition some listen and some do not. Every time we change vibrations and increase our light, as we are in 2012 the human point of perception changes and new truths, feelings and wisdom is adopted, spread your compassion in 2012.

□□

3. CULPABILITY is not MORALITY

CULPABILITY is placing blame, guilt, fault or responsibility. In human law the judge or courts place culpability on the individual or group and decide a monetary value for any injury or injustice. Your continuing freedom or NOT is also decided for you. When you are considered retarded or not responsible there is no culpability. These are externally applied judgments or ways to force an individual or group to behave morally and fairly with each other, which is needed when dealing with duality and the dark ones found on earth.

Individuals with low self worth, criminals and the dark ones are dangerous to themselves and others and cannot be trusted to be compassionate with them self and others. There is no way to force them to go light or behave fairly. You can force the dark to lie and deceive you but the morals are the same. When they appear to be fair and compassionate it is generally to set you up for another trick, lie or deception to come.

Morality or moral behavior of the individual NEEDS to be based on what the individual actually THINKS not what they say or do. As we move into higher vibrations we will be able to read everyone's thoughts. We will not be able to hide from our own thoughts. We will not be able to lie to our self or others. Converting your old judgment and blame thinking to "compassionate think" is a bit tricky but very doable.

Aligning internal thought patterns to "give and receive only compassion" takes desire and some skill and attention. You need to release the way human law functions first because all will see the lies and deceptions including you. The duality definition of right and wrong is not applicable in higher vibrations because human law takes responsibility for the person's thought, behavior and then tries to control them. All of these actions go against the universal law of allowing.

In higher vibrations you must be compassionate with you first and responsible for you at the same time. When you master being compassionate and responsible to you first that will easily transfer into love and service to others. When you are addicted, dissociated or blaming another you are not responsible for you and show NO COMPAS- SION. You have allowed or forced another to be responsible for you. Only dark ones deny their responsibilities.

Spiritual wisdom and the ascension process is an unending process. Wisdom is an evolutionary process not a destination or endpoint. It is done BY YOU and for you. A wise individual in a group of wise individuals makes for a wise collective consciousness. Know that you have experienced different phases of the ascension process many times before in a multitude of locations and realities. Spiritual knowledge must be integrated and USED.

Knowing how to swim and swimming are two different things. Knowing universal law and living the laws are different. To facilitate your growth, healing and culpability you need to maintain clear thought, be responsible for your thoughts and stay in the now moment all the time. That will be how you can joyfully and comfortably move into higher vibrations and unity by being culpable for you.

The universal law of PERPETUAL TRANSMUTATION of ENERGY is that all humans have the power to change the conditions in their life. Raising your vibration is hard work. You need you to stay in your biology and focus your thoughts. We all have the skill set to do that. The imbalances you attracted to you because of your attachment to an agenda, thing or person have to be UNDONE or uncreated by you also. With all freedoms and increased aware- ness there are responsibilities to create win-win-win for all involved.

□□

UNIVERSAL LAW of ACTION

The universal law of ACTION means the individual must ACT first to start their thoughts moving in another direction. Make the many little moves in thought that prove your commitment to a different direction. Then your soul aspects will line up synchronicities in the vibration or level of compassion that you actually function in. For those that have chosen the light or higher vibrations by 2012 and are committed and able to be more light than dark, proving that to your self with action will be the way to go.

The energies on earth now are very supportive and with any new freedom come responsibilities. Changes in higher vibrations DO NOT happen with physical force. Force, conquering or control even of your own biology is what dark uses and goes against universal law. The individual learning or unfolding the higher truths for them self is divine will.

The universal law of DIVINE MANIFESTATION is win- win-win-win to benefit all involved and harm to none. Any harm to another in the process or outcome of manifestation is not DIVINE and carries karmic debt.

The universal law of FREEWILL is divine will granting each entity the right to direct and pursue his or her life so long as he or she does not violate the same right of others. A right that excludes the rights of others is NOT DIVINE.

With your actions and thoughts develop win-win-win strategies. When interacting with another individual, concept or idea, create "win-win" OPTIONS for them and you because all the situations and individuals you are interact- ing with presently are issues in your reality that need resolution. When you present a win-win option FREQUENTLY the other will not go along with it. Not to worry, just allow that. Your responsibility was to offer a win-win. They are ALLOWED to direct and pursue their life the way they want to. Remember that 46.16% on earth are MORE DARK than light and moving to greater darkness so they are not following universal law, but you are.

Historically and in many lifetimes our interaction was win-lose or lose-lose energy and now we can turn that around for the self by being compassionate. When you consistently offer the win option to one that you forced or controlled historically you can change your personal history. By changing our interactions permanently in the now moment to win-win-win we can rewrite and heal that type of interaction for OUR SELF now and in concurrent lifetimes.

For example if person "A" always controlled individual "B" in 24 concurrent experiences and in present time. Then person "A" CHANGED her thoughts and is now ALLOWING individual "B" to do as they wish all the time. Then the 24 concurrent experiences would change and be rewritten for "A" in all the experiences. "B" could stop being a victim or she can easily locate another predator. It is "B's" freewill to decide the direction of her thoughts.

When things get rewritten like they are for "A" the process will make "A" feel foggy or spacey for a few days until the rewriting is completed. The old dense vibrations or the DNA patterns in concurrent lives will be shifted to higher vibrations. When one aspect gathers spiritual wisdom all your other aspects learn the spiritual wisdom also, it is a win-win-win.

Another example is you have been the victim of predator "C" for 25 lifetimes and today you decide "no more" and you walk away and allow NO ONE to bully you or steal your light anymore and you love yourself enough so you do not bully another weak or dependent one. You can rewrite the past 25 lifetimes with you being on equal footing with "C." Now predator "C" will still be a predator but you will not be their victim. Without you being their victim their life will change some or they can find another terrorist.

A GRAND SYNCHRONICITY For example, there is a marriage with two children going darker with no option to change the family members and one is dying of cancer. Enter individual "E" is an adult outside the marriage that starts up a relationship with "S" an adult inside the marriage relationship that has been numb since mom used him as a sexual toy as an infant and during the childhood.

"E" was used as a sexual toy by her mom also.

"E" and "S" have the potential to heal many dark choices in past concurrent lives and the soul aspects create synchronicities to facilitate many light choices. The invisible aspects of the other spouse and children create synchronicities for them to facilitate many light choices for them. They line up choices for them to meet and bond with individuals lighter than they are to help heal some of the darker choices the other spouse and children have made in concurrent lifetimes.

That is how a divorce or separation can be set up to be a win-win-win. Universal law does not condone STAGNANT relationships of any sort. Human marriage vows or contracts or work contracts to force or control one or more parties are not spiritual law or wisdom. They are little human dark law about what you owe and need to sacrifice.

The universal principle of ENTHUSIASM is that new thoughts make you feel enthusiastic. A new belief always shows up to challenge an old one. New thoughts increase enthusiasm. Stagnating in old patterns and relationships result in robotic thought and lost enthusiasm. Stagnation depletes our energy and light disconnecting us from our soul aspects.

Your personal Akashi record or history is not a stack of lifetimes to be read or ordered. Those reading past or con- current lives are reading energies that all sit on the surface and are mixed together. Unresolved issues are on the top or most prominent. Every single lifetime, biology, talent or skill you have ever had and your weaknesses and strengths are all there in a quantum state.

For example when you are attached to the belief that you will age in a certain way you will create that. When there's not a conscious effort to change anything currently in your DNA it reproduces what it created before. You remain static and or stagnate and your future holds more of the same fears and phobias for you to continue to experience.

□□

PARADOXES will INCREASE

PARADOX is something that is opposite or different or contradictory from what seems logically to be true with the knowledge we have gathered throughout life. Humans have operated with very limited information and we have been misdirected about a great many things. For example we have been told we are the only life forms and the most advanced life forms in the universe. So when an alien with- out a spaceship comes to help you manifest dinner that may be a paradox to you. When your belief is that there is no such thing as a "green frog" and one sits in front of you, is that a paradox? Is that your ignorance about green frogs? Or do you deny knowing or seeing the green frog exists? Then I guess there is no paradox for you.

Our journey has been millions of years long and we have forgotten a huge amount and how to access that in- formation. Most paradoxes are a result of our ignorance of what is true in the now moment or present time. What was true just a moment ago may not be true right now. And what was false a moment ago may no longer be false. For example when we discover that other planets are teeming with life that is far more advanced than the humans on earth. Is that a paradox or ignorance?

For example when you ask your soul aspect "how much light you carry?" and they say 60%. That would be true for that moment. When you ask your soul aspect "How much light do I carry most of the time?" they may give a different percentage. Or if you have more than one personality they can give a number for each of your multiple personalities.

Loops or cycles of similar events would be time travel if time were linear. Linear time is an illusion and for the 3rd dimension only. Time is in loops of similar events. For example you could be living in 2012 and during the time of Christ con- currently. The one you focused your attention on would be the one you were living in the now moment. That would be your time travel. Time and space gave those in the 3rd dimension the illusion of separation from others and your higher vibrating soul aspects. When we believe that to be true then that illusion is reinforced by us.

The universal principle of PARADOX recognizes the movement of energies in four dimensions happening simultaneously. Cause and Effect, Inertia, Microcosm and Macrocosm and Vibration come together in a collision at a certain point. Paradox seen on a flat plane is like a stone dropped in a stream with the ripples moving out. Paradox in a CUBED space would create VIBRATIONS in all directions. Paradox touches high levels of vibration and dense levels of vibration at the same time or SIMULTANEOUSLY and the entire area appears to be alive with movement. Whatever is said about one level holds true or is untrue for all levels.

A paradox is two swirling portals merging partially or overlapping each other to create a new reality or truth, in the area overlapping each other. One portal is higher vibrating and imparts new information to the lower vibrating portal. These paradox portals are all over the earth now.

The paradox is that each vibration creates a different manifestation. For example when you are vibrating slow and operating with dark thoughts of control and force the law of attraction brings you experiences of BEING con- trolled and forced physically and or spiritually. When you carry more light than dark and are being compassionate with yourself the law of attraction brings like energy and experiences to you and life can be joyful instead of fearful.

Whatever is said about one level of vibration holds true or is untrue for all levels. BUT in low vibrations it can look very distorted and even cruel and painful. A great many of our lives were lived trapped in fear and suffering until we died and that held us in the lower 4th dimension to reincarnate into another life of fear and suffering.

Consider PASSION for example, passionate love or hate is strong focused emotion and energy. Rage is DIS- CORDANT energy and a low vibration. Passion is a response of harmony with a high vibration. When similar frequencies band together a group mind set is formed and reinforced. Measured in universal energy it is the same. Passionate hate may get you killed or tortured physically or spiritually. Many in the lower 4th dimension are holding very passionate beliefs that keep them stuck in darkness. Hate is a slow vibration carrying little if any light. When you die holding the belief that someone needs to be punished for a wrong they did to you that goes against universal law and you will stay stuck in that pattern of dark beliefs until your thoughts change.

The paradox here is that your soul agreed to have the experience you had to gain spiritual wisdom. You failed to gather the spiritual wisdom and will keep repeating that experience until you "get it" and that may feel like an eternity for a slow learner. You need to find another point of view to discern what you experienced. See it an- other way. Show compassion for you and your challenging learning experience.

Increased levels of electromagnetic light energy from the higher dimensions are now flowing within all of us to increase our clarity of thought. Those that are "more dark than light" fighting awareness are not able to handle the light and they are choosing to leave their biology. As our pockets of density or dark are being transmuted they will be brought to our conscious awareness. People and circumstances will be magnetized to us that mirror the vibration we emanate. If you can observe these things with detachment and OWN them they will transmute or clear up quickly. If you grab hold and engage yourself in drama of any kind about what you experience, the things brought to your awareness will attach to you and hold you in that low vibration. Fighting them in anyway or giving them your attention is ALWAYS joining them and attaching you to their vibration.

Another paradox is our belief that what we think doesn't matter and can't hurt anyone. Thoughts don't just disappear after we think them they live on. Thoughts have specific weight, texture, density and emotional charge. Our thought as individuals dictate the amount of light we can carry and emanate. As a group our dark or light thoughts bond and cluster together with all the other thoughts people emanate of the same vibration. Ugly thoughts come highly charged (very passionate) and wrapped in highly magnetic emotions. That does affect everyone in the group or on the earth.

The paradox is that we believed we were separate and could think and do what we wanted to do to others without it coming back to us. That could also be called denial, ignorance or self-deception.

Living in linear time means you WORK HARD and WAIT for your creations and money for all the hard work you did. In higher vibrations when you create you think and feel it as it instantly manifests. The hot fudge Sunday is in your hand, did you remember a spoon? There is no need for recognition or financial reward for your creations and there is no need for hard work.

Another paradox is that without time and space there will be only now and here. We are HERE because we never left. We are here because we bi and tri locate. We are here because we are everywhere. We have acted as a portal so that the aspects of our soul that vibrates higher than humans can experience life in 3rd dimension vicariously. Now our soul aspects that vibrate higher than the human can act as an inner portal for us to experience higher vibrations.

□□

RELEASE SUFFERING and SELF HATE

The 3rd dimension set of rules is relatively DARK and inflexible based on multiple lies, illusion and secrets. Lies about what is real and who we are because those are the rules of darkness and unconsciousness. In 3rd and 4th dimension there are LOOPS of SIMILAR EVENTS or repeated thought patterns over and over again UNTIL you gather the wisdom to evolve out of that particular loop. When we focus our attention on the past we recreate it in present time. But to move out of 3rd and 4th dimension the lies and YOUR self deceptions need to be exposed, owned and the "emotional charge" or your personal suffering needs to be released or integrated by you.

Initially we planned our experiences to follow the rules of the 4th dimension BUT we made so many little dark and fearful choices we wound up in the 3rd dimension calibrating our consciousness to Beta brainwaves. Reality is perceived as being outside of you creating separation, opposites, linear time, and death and forgetting. Beta brainwaves are associated with aggression, survival and sexual impulses. The belief system and MORALITY created for the little human is that of being a victim and everything good or bad comes from outside of you. "What you gain I loose." Suffering allows awareness.

DIMENSIONS are consciousness and each dimension has a FIXED vibration or awareness with a different game and set of rules for those choosing to play and create there. Dimensions have different THEMES or purposes with different vibrations that all interact with each other. They can move and shift like our thoughts do. Dimensions are distinct event sites and there are infinite numbers of sites and particular planes of consciousness or spiritual light not stacked like pancakes.

Dimensions do not occupy time or space because they are states of consciousness available to anyone who vibrates in resonance with the specific frequency and opportunities available in each dimension.

The first three universal wholes, 1st, 2nd and 3rd dimension are given order by the 4th dimension of time. The universal whole is a self-created, self-sustaining MENTAL creation or holograph. 5th dimension is not a hologram it is a reality where you integrate all you learned in 1st to 4th lower vibrating worlds. Holographic realities are places of learning in the lower dimensions. When our thoughts and emotions become fearful the lowered consciousness re- turns to lower vibrations it is simply a matter of resonance NOT punishment. Our reality is a result of our vibration or alignment with universal law.

The 4th dimension is a needed short-lived stepping-stone to move into 5th dimension. In 4th dimension you need to know what you think and align that with spiritual truths or universal law. Alpha brain waves are normal when we are relaxed. In an Alpha state you perceive both the "outside world" and "your inside world" simultaneously. 4th dimension is always in present time, less dense with greater possibilities and less structure. You can observe events and gather information with detachment. Shifts in your thinking are subtle and easier. Gaia and many humans (not all), cetaceans, animals, plants and the mineral kingdom moved to 4th dimension in 2001 working their way to the 5th dimension. 4th dimension is the emotional aura of Gaia.

While in the 4th dimension you have memories, dreams and experiences of your parallel realities or concur- rent lifetimes. 4th dimension is divided into 3 levels with entities having various agendas from outright interference with our development to assistance and blessings.

LOWER 4th dimension is or was souls emanating and stuck in fear and darkness creating "static" making it difficult for us to receive messages from higher vibrations. HELL is not a place it is a resonance of the lower 4th dimension and limited thought. There are earthbound souls still addicted to substance and sexual abuse and they are filled with despair and hopelessness.   They can and do SUCK energies from low vibrating humans, possess humans and encourage humans to do some pretty nasty things like hate them self. The 4th dimension and aura of planet earth has dark and light patches or pockets just as humans do. There are many places of light and power on earth along with places of injustice, cruelty, fear and anger. The dark ones in the lower 4th dimension needed someone lighter to help him or her "go to the light" or "cross over" because dark repels light.

The HIGHER ASTRAL level of the 4th dimension is close to the fifth dimension with many guides and teachers. In-between 4th and 5th dimension is the Great Void. Dimensions one through four are on the physical or astral side of the Great Void and 5th to 8th dimensions are on the spiritual side of the Void.

5th dimension is balancing light and dark into one-ness. We can self-correct our dark thinking. Your attachment to anything or anyone that carries a resonance lower than the fifth dimension (like a dark family member) or your "dark pattern of behavior" like "blaming or victimization" will diminish your ability to stay in higher vibrations and make it difficult for you to experience more than one reality at a time. Whole brain thinking allows instant acceptance, integration and understanding of all information.

In the 5th dimension you don't have to GO anywhere. Your answers and experiences come to you based on your focus and vibration. You create with light patterns and frequencies. You apply sound and color and geometric shapes. Light travels faster increasing harmonic resonance and colors from 72 to 123 to help activate genetic restructuring and more skills.

Calibrated to the 5th and 6th dimension you function in THETA brain waves and experience only your "inside world" with an awareness of your biology and with practice, you are able to connect to the awareness of Gaia and her essences and experiences. Calibrated with delta cycles you ONLY experience your inside world or spiritual aware- ness or soul aspect with little connection to the biology. You are also able to experience Galactic awareness and are primarily attached to your higher dimensional bodies as you travel the Universe as your essence.

☐☐

4. PHYSICS of CREATING

PHYSICS is concerned with the properties of matter and energy and the way they work. How heat, light, radiation, sound, electricity, magnetism work and the structure of atoms. Human physicists have not factored in how human thought or CONSCIOUSNESS restructures matter all the time. Matter on the quantum level starts forming around our thought to create what we think about. Thought creates the very small and the very large including galaxies. The things and people we think about and give our energy to we are attached to mentally and emotionally. Our attachments create our world or reality and attraction reinforces the thought or creation bringing us more of the same.

QUANTUM PHYSICS or theory or mechanics is a mathematical equation of the interaction of matter with energy on the small scale of "atoms and subatomic" particles. Using a wave you can create probabilities to accurately predict the physical behavior of different systems. Light and other matter regularly changes from waves to particles. Light changes to particles when humans observe it. Light and matter quanta behave differently when humans WATCH them and quantum scientists have shown that the

THOUGHTS and expectations of the experimenter have a direct effect on outcomes. Quantum energy deals with potentials not absolute attributes.

QUANTA or the singular quantum is the SMALLEST unit of any physical entity. For example a photon is a single quantum of light or one "light quantum." Our DNA on the quanta level carries our lineage from other planets like the Pleiades and other areas of the Universe.

A PHOTON is a quantum of light that can gather thoughts, has memory, thinks, evolves and does NOT have a past or future. Photons are self-directing to any need in the now moment and can transfer energy from one end of the universe to the other end and not be diminished because they travel in a vacuum at the speed of light and have both wave and particle properties. Photons carry all electromagnetic radiation and wavelengths, gamma rays, X-rays, ultraviolet light, visible light, infrared light, microwaves, and radio waves.

Photon energy comes into the pineal gland portal to be distributed through out our biology. Photons raise our vibration and consequently wake us up, make us conscious. When you carry 80% light or more you can direct the photon in the now moment. Around 2030, photon energy will be the predominant energy changing the magnetic field on earth so no existing technology will work. Our cars, radios, televisions, planes and computers won't work when the magnetic field is altered that much. After the great shift photons will REPLACE electricity, as photons are a form of infinite electromagnetic energy.

Our consciousness or awareness restructures matter and large objects the same way it does with quanta. The quantum energy of the galaxy or the physics is not standardized. Galaxies are similar with slight differences de- pending on what is at the center of each galaxy. The push / pull system is found in the middle of all galaxies and planets including earth. The push / pull system is a double event. Everything in our physics comes in pairs. The push / pull system of multidimensional energy surges back and forth to energize our holograms. There are two holes; one black hole and one hole not VISIBLE to most humans.   These multidimensional strings of force connect themselves to the other galaxies, weaving in and out of their centers stringing all the galaxies together. There is always a symmetry and purpose in our universe. When you look down the middle of the galaxies in the universe you will see the symmetry that looks like a Mandela. Galaxies have something in the middle that is gravity based and everything moves around the center as one. All objects around a gravitational pull seek their orbits based upon their mass and speed. That's why all the planets have different orbits.

DARK MATTER follows multidimensional law it is quantum. Spaceships align their routes along the push pull multidimensional energy. This is pointed out in the star trek movie Star Trek XI, 2009. When you are in alignment with the dimensions you are in round time. You travel using the push / pull system that creates space highways or worm- holes. The vortex technology takes you from one reality to another. 17 wormholes or space highways have been dis- covered in our galaxy so far. Several of these space high- ways connect to other galaxies. A propelled spacecraft moves through dimensions and not to planets. The cosmic pulse within spiral galaxies forms a creation pattern spiral that lends it self to physical matter and duality.

The GALACTIC GRID or COSMIC LATTICE is the energy we have on, in and around the earth. The lattice holds this illusion together, which is in transition now. It is an omnipotent source of energy. All the grids are formatted to allow all within them to expand creatively. Each galaxy has a collective conscious- ness or a living energy field that is the sum of its entire species. The universal mind is awake and aware.

Human nature is becoming more benevolent. First the INDIVIDUAL becomes more compassionate creating a more compassionate collective consciousness. As we own and understand our past limited thoughts we change our future. Individually we are becoming increasingly peaceful and less upset. Yes, there are always those that are unbalanced and uncontrollable. The evolution of consciousness is happening without leadership or a hierarchy or force. The higher vibrations wake people up putting them into the position of needing to choose the beliefs they want to follow. No more following the leader or biggest bully. By divine intervention the Galactic society is rendering the dark and Illuminati harmless.

VIBRATIONS are MEASURABLE in HERTZ as Andrew Kemp has studied and shown. Our physical body or plane vibrates at zero to 1,624 Hertz. Our ETHERIC bodies that surround the biology vibrate at 1,624 to 2,245 Hertz.

When we experience physical and emotional trauma especially in childhood our essence moves into a small band of vibration just above or outside our etheric bodies. The aspects of our core self reside there and vibrate at 2,245 to 2,345 Hertz until it can return to the biology. The essence did not move in time or space but INCREASED its vibration to just outside the physical and etheric spectrums while the biology withstands trauma and LOW vibration or resonance. When the core trauma is healed the essence can drop resonance to the etheric bodies or the biology. Sometimes a child needs to leave the abusive home or their handlers for the core self to feel safe enough to reenter the biology.

HIGHER dimensions are at 2,345 to 11,268 Hertz and that is where we are moving if we carry enough light or vibrate fast enough.

SOUL vibration is 11,268 Hertz and on up unless the soul aspects have gone dark decreasing their vibration and awareness with the human they followed into darkness.

□□

YOUR ATTACHMENTS do your CREATING

We all have the power to transform whatever we choose. All of our creations individual and collectively created are always TEMPORARY. Each creation demonstrates the thoughts and feelings of those who created the experience, the event or condition. No matter how horrific or wonderful a creation it is. Removing your mental and emotional attachment makes it go away. If you have a wound and you keep licking it or giving it your focus and energy you keep dragging the past into present time.

The law of PERPETUAL TRANSMUTATION of ENERGY says we all have the power to change the conditions of our life. Raising your vibration is hard work. You need to stay present and conscious in your biology and focus your thoughts. Instead of inflexibility, disdain, and righteous- ness consider kindness, gentleness, and compassion with your self and others to resolve wounds and issues. Forced agreements or plans made in anger or frustration create resentment creating failure in the long run that encourages retaliation. Lack has been an artificially created illusion for humanity. This planet can easily provide abundance for all. Allowing is the knowledge that everything is as it ought to be. Everyone is on his or her own individual path to spiritual wisdom.

Attachment to the outcome of anything like what a spouse or child may do or not do goes against you allowing. Even when the other person is being self-destructive that is their creation and their path you need to allow.

Concern your self with something pleasant and enjoyable for you.

Prayer, mantras and rituals are used to ask another to do what you need to do for the self. That is giving your power away. Each of us must create and focus on our own thoughts, awareness and reality. That is why being a leader or a follower goes against the universal law of allowing. Force and saving others is really you trying to create YOUR reality against the will of the other. That helps none and keeps all of you in a low vibrating darkness.

Those individuals carrying mid ranges of light (40 to 60%) find mantras, prayers and rituals comforting and offer them the illusion of community or the feeling of being SPECIAL. Some rituals are just fun like Christmas and Hanukah. Those that carry a lot of light and have a high vibration find that mantras, prayers and rituals get in the way and are not appropriate.

New thoughts make you feel enthusiastic and new beliefs always show up to challenge old ones. Stagnating in old patterns and relationships result in robotic thought and lost enthusiasm. Stagnation depletes our energy and light disconnecting us from our soul aspects. When there's not a conscious effort to change anything currently in your DNA or aura it reproduces what it created before. You keep recreating what you have. You remain static and stagnate and your future holds more of the same predispositions, fears and phobias you have always had. JOY and INNER PEACE increases with deeper connection of the little human to their soul aspects giving up the human free will for living in divine will. The way you feel about WHO you are on the inside, what you do, and what you have created creates your happiness.

□□

YOUR THOUGHTS create Your MATRIX

The MATRIX or ILLUSION we have lived in for the past 12 thousand years is a carefully crafted program of beliefs designed to benefit the few on top that run and reinforce the slave mentality we have embraced in order to keep surviving one more day. Dissenters get discredited or accidently die. Most of our spiritual, religious teachings and social pressure ask us to follow their concept of a greater power that will save us a power that lives in our matrix. All our fairytales, television dramas and many books present ONE super hero rescuing the group. If that is what you are waiting for you will NEVER get out of this matrix. You evolve out of this illusion individually with you and your soul aspects or stay in the matrix with your attachments and dark behavior patterns. The group of individuals that has taken responsibility for their thoughts and have com- passion for the self will hold a space for you while you wait to be rescued.

This is the time for waking up and becoming aware of the choices we made consciously or unconsciously. People are no longer willing to "put up and shut up" allowing the secret political government to conduct business as usual. The reforms promised need to be instituted. Our rise in consciousness makes it impossible for those recently brought to power to go back to the old ways. There is a deep need for meaningful interaction, honesty and trans- parent interactions between government and its citizens.

Enabling and allowing the dark ones to "suck the life out of you" will trap you in the matrix. Individually we need to take responsibility for our creations. Stop caretaking and just hold a space for others. HOLDING a SPACE is being supportive or increasing someone's awareness when they ask for it. When they are ready to act give support and in- formation. If their focus is on their immediate "little human WOUND or an act of vengeance or gossip" wait, they are not ready yet. WAIT for them to get clarity on the bigger spiritual picture or lesson they CHOSE to be in the middle of. You honor their choice to work with that lesson as long as they want to.

Attachment to the outcome of anything a friend, neighbor or grand parent may do or not do goes against the law of ALLOWING. Even when the other person hurts them self or is doing a "good thing" like caretaking that is their creation and their path that you need to allow them to follow. When you are controlling, manipulative, worried, guilty, angry, vengeful or focusing on the other person you are ATTACHED and TRAPPED in the 3rd dimensional matrix of control.

Over the last two decades the struggle continues be- tween the dark that wants to keep us enslaved and the light working to free us by divine decrees. The light Galactic society has intervened many times on humanities behalf. Various secret governments have maintained vast networks of underground and underwater bases that the Galactic community has recently dismantled. The dark has lost thousands of their research scientists and technicians. The law enforcement agencies are getting ready to arrest thousands of individuals in the top of the dark ones. Televised trials will begin soon similar to the Nuremberg trials.

The dark's goal was to reduce the earth's population by nearly 90% with their vaccines, chemtrails, toxic genetically modified food, weapons and police brutality but that will not stop the SPIRITUAL awakening that is in process. Europe's dark ones are having a meltdown they are fight- ing and turning on each other and in the process exposing their corruption and deceit with each other and the people they used instead of serving.

November 11, 2011 humans and Gaia moved spiritually away from human law and into observing universal law on this planet. Give and receive only compassion. The dark ones are no longer running things but many are still in denial and throwing tantrums.

November 16, 2011 the light galactic community put a stop to the broadcasting of the ELF, Extremely Low Frequency waves at 50–80 Hz put out by the illuminati or the elite few that actually have run our world and us. The dark broadcasted a constant stream of ELF waves through all our airways to prevent us from communication with our self and our own thoughts. Now it will be easier to commune with your essence. With the higher vibration on earth waking people up and the dark ones loosing control of their many secrets and endless illegal activities our life is in process of changing.

The planet and the people living on it are to act as one unit supporting each other. GAIA is the SOUL or consciousness of earth and is a living, sentient, breathing being with innate intelligence like us. She is able to converse with all life on earth. The earth hologram was created ap- proximately five billion years ago. Gaia is the human's sup- port system emotionally, physically and spiritually and we are to be that for her. For the past 12 thousand years she and her inhabitants have had a dark bias in 1987 she was at neutrality. Gaia is at 95% light as of Dec 2011. Her winds of change for this ascension started around 1914 just as humanities change did.

The earth, many humans, cetaceans, animals, plants and the mineral kingdom moved to the 4th dimension in 2001. 4th dimension is the emotional aura of Gaia and was divided into 3 levels. In March 2011 the lower 4th dimension stopped existing because her vibration was higher than the lower 4th dimension. By the November of 2012 the 4th dimension will dissipate.
Historically, when humans did not have biology or when we slept or between lifetimes our "dark soul aspects" HUNG out in the lower 4th dimension. There they played out all sorts of games, battles and energy wars.

There were earthbound souls still addicted to substance, sexual abuse and filled with despair and hopelessness. They could and did SUCK energy from low vibrating humans, possess humans and encouraged humans to be unethical.

The illuminati or generational Satanists that also controlled the earth would possess other illuminati family members still in biology. All the dark soul aspects without biology that were holding the lower 4th dimension and consequently the earth in a lower slower dark vibration have been given some awareness or spiritual wisdom and moved into portals of greater light for them. This has helped raise earth's vibration considerably. This also stopped those souls from possessing humans with biology. Our soul aspects still have memories, dreams and experiences of parallel realities or concurrent lifetimes in the 4th dimension.

The humans on earth committed to unconsciousness or dark are at 46% as of January 1, 2012. As they lose their biology they are being moved off the earth's crystalline grid and into other spaces that match their vibration in the universe. They are no longer calibrated to the earth's frequency. At this time the dark humans with biology that are committed to being unaware of the light are rapidly dying off. The speed of their death depends on the individual's biological weaknesses.

Light vibrating souls and rainbow souls are now FLOODING the crystalline grid around the earth and will need biology to carry out the raising and stabilization of Gaia's vibration. The new soul aspect hangs out with the "parents to be" that match their vibration. The first few weeks or months the fetus is in the womb the soul aspect has not attached to the biology. When and if the soul attaches and the fetus is aborted the expecting mother may experience some depression over the loss of the "spiritual purpose" that baby was to have for the mother.

Unconditional love is ever present in our universe and has detachment, friendship, compassion and constructive purpose. Not until you carry 60% or more light can you start loving you and accept unconditional love. With self-love wisdom and compassion replace ignorance and judgment. Self-love is a REQUIREMENT for you taping into the cosmic flow of unconditional love. Calm you're little human down and use emotional detachment without doubt, fear, victimization or judgment or a lust for power, control, attention or anger. As we move into alignment with universal law and your soul aspects you become calmer, heal faster and move into present time. The invisible realm can be more supportive and proactive in frustrating the dark ones in your life after you have decided to act with com- passion for you first. The universal law of ACTION means you must ACT first to start the ball rolling. Make the many little moves to get things rolling and prove your commitment to the direction you want to move in. Then your soul aspects will line up synchronicities for you in the level of compassion you currently function in.

Believing in anyone or anything outside of you keeps you entrained to this slave matrix. Attaching yourself to anyone, even a family member or anything like a group or idea outside of you keeps you trapped in this illusion. Your thoughts or your refusal to think for yourself creates and recreate your reality. Is your reality inside or outside the matrix?

☐☐

5. WE need to STEP UP and take ACTION

The nuttiness of the few remaining holdouts of the Illuminati throwing tantrums about loss of their ill-gotten gains is encouraging people to STEP UP to the plate! Batter up! Believe CHANGE is a serious possibility as you continuously demonstrate compassion for you and expect fair treatment from your leaders and bankers, your family and friends. Our governments have never had the people's best interest as a top priority. The proof and Information is generally not found in our controlled media, but can be found on the Internet. Seek and thou shall find. Knock and the door shall open. People are posting the Facts and proof on the Internet. They are actively engaged in creating aware- ness. This awareness is resulting in action and change. Your discernment is always needed because even in higher vibrations or resonance you get all the information it is not sorted out for you. Your job is to sort through and discern for yourself the information to use for your needs.

Benjamin Fulford: Neil Keenan and Keith Scott say, World Governments are coming to understand how the Global Banking System run by the illuminati is systematically looting entire economies through theft, fraud, subterfuge, deception and manipulation that in turn forces Governments to raise taxes the citizens have to pay. The days of moving public income to the private side of the ledgers of the banks while they move their PRIVATE LIABILITIES to the public side of the ledgers are almost over. White Drag- on Society members developed and presented a plan that calls for forcing banks to work according to their Charters, and bankers who fail to comply will face the consequences of their actions. In America, it has been estimated that the US Debt could be eliminated in less than four years through this one device.

Taxes could be driven down to their lowest level since the beginning of the nineteenth century. Clean up the trading markets of banks and ensure money goes where it is supposed to go. The countries that have already decided their assets within the Global Accounts System shall be brought under proper control have also decided that Keenan and Scott, the men who have defined where the problems really lie. They have fearlessly moved to resolve these problems. They are also the men who will oversee the accounts. We are on the cusp of a whole new era with integrity and honesty.

It is time to legally put the criminals out of action, arrest and confine them where they can do no more harm. Then we need to focus our attention on the activities aimed at destroying our health and wellbeing. We need to find and put in place a bunch of technology that has been hidden from us that could easily clean the air, land, and water, and provide free electricity.

The Light Galactic society is helping humans deal with the darkness that ran our world. They want to peaceably let the people on earth know they exist and are helping guide our transition or shift we are in the middle of. They have many counselors, special liaison and action teams all over the planet. Key dark individuals and corporations are rapidly being reduced to nothing. The dark-controlled media has spent decades making alien's something to fear and fight. In our own families the darkest ones are generally the parent or grandparent that try to control you and keep you uninformed. The transitional governments that are being created are dedicated to the people's welfare. Punishment of criminals is not to last long and capital punishment is not an option. A nuclear option does not exist.

When mentioning ALIENS or EXTRATERRESTRIALS or even the humans on earth our government doesn't concern itself with the spiritual aspect or needs of an entity. Technically we are all extraterrestrial beings because we all came from someplace else. Our governments have prevented the masses from having access to credible evidence it has, of and about extraterrestrial life. They do not want us to know about the agreements the governments have entered into with the DARK aliens, the Greys, the reptilians and others that live here, work with us and visit us. Our governments sold us out for their personal gain and to the people's detriment consistently. Governments are to change from authoritarian to be more of overseers of many creative solutions. All the people's voices are heard and honored.

Higher vibrating or light extraterrestrials do not trust our governments but do work with light individuals or small organizations. There is a movement on earth to get the USA government to release their secrets about aliens and extraterrestrials. http://www.exopolitics.org

Extraterrestrials and humans both are physical and spiritual entities with immense talents and capabilities. The amount of information both can process each second is considerable. We are all bombarded with data from our various physical realities and from the innumerable spiritual realms we inhabit. As a newborn we all had the ability to be telepathically connected to our entire family, community and the universe. The newborns with souls are keep- ing their skill of telepathy not allowing adults to talk them out of it.

□□

FEAR CONTROLS anything out of BALANCE

YOUR thought and emotion makes you conscious and aware. When your thought and emotion stay in the vibration of unconditional love you can travel and live in higher dimensions or vibrations. That low vibration or matrix of power and control were run with the energy of fear and unbalance. Living and operating in fear is not comfortable or nice when your dark thoughts and emotions return to YOU as rapidly as you send them out. In higher vibrations that is what happens. The law of attraction becomes painful and rather uncomfortable. You learn or suffer.

You being angry or upset or impatient or judgmental is what the law of attraction brings more of, FOR YOU to experience. You demanding that the world be the way YOU want it. The way it is comfortable for you, brings into your life, people that want the world to be the way THEY want it. Even a slight change in the frequency or vibration of your thought or feelings, changes YOUR reality and experiences. When you slip into the past of lower frequencies like worry, doubt, judgment or fear your vibration drops. FEAR prevents you from taking in information from your soul aspect or any higher awareness. In fear you move to the reptilian brain of survival. Your thoughts of fear become the prison you create and maintain for you. When YOU no longer feel fear and YOU REFUSE to own another persons fear you can open your own prison door.

The journey from fear to love and compassion is the largest and hardest journey we ever have to make. Unbalanced thought is the result of negative and verbal assaults we sustained as children or in concurrent lives making us shut down our hearts and minds unable to love and have compassion for our self. To survive we have conditioned our self to seek EXTERNAL approval from family members, leaders and each other. Keeping humans in fear and ignorance makes a compliant servant or slave.

When your brain and mind are like a large room you have thrown bits and pieces of thoughts and different awareness's in without sorting or grouping similar thoughts together you have a large pile of chaos and no way to develop a thought or direction for YOU. You aren't focused long enough on any single thought to develop it or make sense of it. Get to work organizing your thoughts and prioritizing them now or the chaos in your mind will become increasingly more painful to you as our frequency rises. As the planet vibrates higher and a great deal more information gets dropped in your awareness you will feel very CONFUSED.

The BRAIN in our biology is used as a processing center or transformer to step down energy from our soul aspects and the DNA around us. Our brain is used to keep the biology alive in this dimension and this lifetime only. The brain dies with the biology; it is not our consciousness, awareness or intuition. Awareness lives in our mental body that surrounds the biology. The right hemisphere of the brain receives multidimensional information very quickly as pictures and provides large volumes of raw data.

The left hemisphere has allowed us to pretend to be a very limited human having a past, present and future. The brain is logical and takes in information slowly always needing repetition. The brain has had limited awareness of all that we are. At this time the two halves of the brain are being rewired to work together again so the brain can process the fact that we are multidimensional and can rapidly receive all the new information or knowingness available to us. When we release what we are accustom to, there may be sadness, grieving and crying for what we thought we were, we release or leave. Have great compassion for yourself during these times of change.

Our CONSCIOUSNESS or awareness is not located in the brain it is found in our mental body or mind that exists in a quantum state around the biology. Our knowingness, intuition, sensory awareness, perceptions or "gut feelings" come from the information surrounding us. That is why we can know or sense in advance when something is about to happen. The brain will know about it when it happens or after it processes what took place. Consciousness is information passed by electrical signals to the field around or the latticework of our DNA that receives and relays information and instructions magnetically. Our DNA inside and out communicates with itself and works together as one unit. This field around us is also a portal OR our aura OR our Merkabah.

A thought and the resulting behavior pattern from any concurrent life keeps recreating itself UNTIL a belief or attitude or association changes your consciousness or awareness.

In a true quantum state time moves in all directions and becomes windows of opportunity or open portals. In round time or time loops the SEQUENCE of events or series of choices build on each other creating an experience with points of separation. An interaction with another has a beginning middle and end points. When loops of similar events intersect with each other the law of attraction brings all the similar experiences together for you to understand the way you think and the results you create with your thoughts. Think angry and your experiences will be angry experiences.

Your present time experience and all the other times you experienced a similar event can be you stuck in an OLD pattern loop again not gathering the wisdom. This is a window of opportunity for you to alter your thought in all those realities and experiences on that chain of similar experiences. Changing your thoughts will change your point of perception. That can rewrite all your past, present and future experiences of similar events.

For example: Each time you hear people "argue about money." You can also hear "arguments about money" from the future, the past, your childhood. You hold certain beliefs about "money arguments" that spring to your aware- ness and will generally dictate YOUR reaction to hearing one more argument about money one more time. Your awareness of your belief about money arguments gives you the opportunity to adopt new points of perception and consequently behaviors in reference to money arguments. When you change a core belief in the now moment PERMANENTLY, it automatically changes all your past and future interactions around "money arguments" for you.

MULTIDIMENSIONAL means there is no specific location or place it is actually an information transfer. Things in their true quantum state are everywhere mixed into the universal soup of oneness and information. This soup of photons or light energy is ever ready to manifest or create in alignment with our thoughts.

MULTIDIMENSIONAL REALITIES are similar and nested all around us allowing easy access to each other and the information they hold. The past, future and concur- rent lives exist as a series of electromagnetic receptors held in the crystalline portion of the physical brain and our mental body around us. These electromagnetic codes are in constant states of flux. We are continuously scripting what happens next. The past is no more fixed than our future is.

☐☐

ENTRAINMENT to CODEPENDENCY

There have been many dark lifetimes of codependency or being the victim and predator for those on earth. Hu- mans have emanated dark and fear for thousands of years so there are many dark soul-to-soul agreements or entrainments you are probably still honoring and triggering that hold you in a band of darkness and low vibration. That keeps you attached to one or more people that chose to stay in their dark patterns. To go lighter you need to break those soul contracts. To change any of those patterns of dark thought the individual human needs to take the lead and commit to breaking that pattern and any DARK soul contracts made in past or concurrent lifetimes.

For example there are three generations of males you honor and revere and they no longer have biology but their soul aspects are very attached to some dark behaviors and addictions that you dabble in also. Because like attracts like they "hang out" with you all the time and strongly influence your beliefs and behavior. That puts the Universal Law of ENTRAINMENT into effect. The law requiring two or more vibrations (the amount of light you carry) existing in the same space MUST combine and adjusts to have one resonance. If you are 60% light generally and your father is 40% light and grandpa is 20% light and great grandpa is 10% you add the 4 percentages up and divide by 4 to get the entrained percentage of light the 4 of you carry when you hang out together, The group operates at around 32% light. With only 32% light you probably have a group of rather angry men or fathers that were abused as children. These men have not crossed over because they are waiting to get VENGEANCE on their abusers. They are waiting for the love and acceptance they never got from dear ole dad. The adult (parent) that abuses their child is wounded, angry and has no compassion for them self.

A wiser spiritual way to go would be to educate these angry wounded men. When you are no longer attached to them or honoring them you go back to your 60% light. Tell these men they need to have compassion for the small child they were that was abused by a dark adult. They need to give the child they were the love and acceptance they never got. By you raising their vibration or awareness enough you can also help them move to a portal of greater light. Ask them if they want to move to greater light and when they say yes; hold your arms in a circle for them to go through to greater light.

The Universal Law of ENTRAINMENT requires that two or more vibrations existing in the same space MUST combine and adjust to have one resonance. For Example, on a scale of 1-10 if your spouse is at 3 and you are at 7 you both are required by the law of entrainment to be at 5. Or when one vibration is overpowering like the photon belt is, that one will pull the other to their level so both would move to 6,7 OR when the dark one is strongest both move to 3,4. "The universal PRINCIPLE of Reconciliation" al- lows different qualities to get unified into similarities. That diminishes differences and decreases conflict to promote commonalities, harmony and balance in all things sharing the same space.

Another mathematical example to explain entrainment is to use a number line with zero at the center and positive numbers on one side and negative numbers on the other side of the number line. A darkness of—3 would need at least a + 3 to neutralize the darkness or to REMIND the darkness that it comes from the light. Dark can return to the light if it chooses to align with universal law but it will take more than just a + 3 in change of thought and behavior to MOVE to the light.

The universal law of entrainment may not seem too important until you take a closer look at all your relation- ships and notice how strongly their entrainment effects you. Consider the effect of the seen and UNSEEN entities and energies in your existence. Even the planet, country and neighborhood you live in affect your entrainment.

Entrainment is having your energetic field overlap another's energy field so that two or more of you can get in sync and feel each other's thoughts and emotions for healing and rebalance. Entrainment can be with all 4 of your bodies, your biology, emotional body, mental body and spiritual body. Or possibly just one or two bodies may overlap for a short period of time. Our soul aspects create entrainments for the human.

Higher vibrations carry no cords they have sharing, detachment, friendship, compassion and constructive purpose. The photon belt and sun entrainment with Gaia and humans is increasing everyone's vibration, information and awareness. The photons WAKE us up by making us FEEL our FEELINGS and that is why many cry more lately. They feel more lately. Being awake and feeling, allows us to make "individual choices" about the direction or entrainment we want to be flowing in. With the higher vibrations feeding tubes or cords are dissolving. For those with less than 50 to 60% light dissolved feeding cords are creating anxiety and confusion in them.

Entrainment is engraved in the fabric of the universe and works in tandem with the law of attraction and allowing. On a planet of free will YOU ALONE "the little human" MUST choose to align with universal law or you default to darker vibrations. There are no superheroes working on your behalf. A group can't do it for you either. There are basically two choices now! Align with light and universal law or DEFAULT to duality and experiencing more of the victim predator suffering cycle. Attachment and feeding is how the dark ones stay alive they literally suck the life out of you.

For example when your belief is that "you cannot live without someone" living or dead you are energetically connected and there is a feeding tube. This is low vibration thought because no ones essence ever leaves. When you can't live without approval or love from a parent or child or someone else you are feeding and saying you do not value you as much as you do another. Low vibrating dark parents siphon LARGE amounts of energy from their children. Even after physical death cords can be fully functional and used by your dead relative or a rejected aspect of you or a dead predator. Cords help you stay connected and en- trained in an emotion or thought pattern of energy. For example "I hate ME" or "I love him" "I hate her" or "I cannot live without..." dislike and intolerance are not useful long-term feelings and create cords that bind. Hanging on to your OLD beliefs and entrainments, ties up some pretty in- tense dark energy like fear, anger, betrayal, guilt or shared beliefs of revenge. Your fondness for the Roman Empire or your lifetime in Atlantis or your dark friends from Pleiades, may have energy cords going to it or them that hold you. Where there is drama there are cords to feed from.

□□

6. CONTRACTS with ALIEN GREYS

Abductions are and have been DONE by the military at times and blamed on aliens. Our governments historically have made contracts with aliens or extraterrestrial Greys that are still in affect. The German government in 1931 was contacted by the Greys but they were committed already to Gizeh intelligence that included Dracos, humans extraterrestrials, dark Pleiadians, Ashtar, Kamagol and Jehovah. They all pretended to be gods. They were and are headquartered under the Gizeh plateau in Egypt. In the early 20th century, the Gizeh intelligence backed Adolf Hitler in Germany and his Rothschild-Windsor sponsors in England.

The Greys taught cloning of humans. They assisted the illuminati to build facilities on the moon and Mars to control and isolate earth even more. They built weapons; particle beam weapons, lasers, nuclear bomb satellites, and anti-matter weapon systems. From the moon they artificially create storms on earth at sea, or over large lakes, and then guide them to a specific target or location by modifying upper atmosphere electrical charges. They can create weather catastrophes all over earth to put us into survival mode and fear. Fear will get us asking for the New World Order to "save us." Just as we did with 9-11 when we lost even more freedoms.

Protection is slavery; a relationship of care taking points that out so clearly. The Illuminati plan was to destroy our world economy and put in place the One World Religion and the One World Order to be forced on us after we asked to be SAVED.

PROBLEM, Reaction and SOLUTION

Problem the dark creates. Reaction from the "victim" they want protection of caretaking from the bully. Solution is that the bully gets to do what it wanted to do in the first place and the victim wouldn't go along with until they went into fear. Then the victim wanted to be SAVED. Like the Nazi's did to Germany.

Apollo 15 discovered portions of the moons crust are radioactive near the Apennine Mountains. Some nuclear waste was brought up there to be reused as a fuel supply for spacecraft the New World Order built that are obsolete now and the tax payer paid for. 53 UFO type spacecraft were built on the moon.

The Greys have cloned their own race into a caste sys- tem like some insects and the reptilians do. The Grey made a contract with United States government May of 1954 to exchange technology and energy sciences for the Greys to study human development, emotions and consciousness and be allowed to stay on Earth. They have studied us the way scientists have studied lab rats. USA became host to the Grey alien race and allied with the Draco's or Illuminati.

Those contracts made by our governments wanting only to build their own power base and control us meant our leaders were aligned with dark and not interested in supporting "the common man and woman." Until very recently the galactic society and the light Andromeda Council couldn't help earth much as a group because our leaders chose the dark for us. That meant ascension had to happen on an INDIVIDUAL basis or not at all. Alien and extraterrestrial Greys are allowed by government CONTRACT to do what they want with us. Many people have brain implants seen on X-Rays and that can be from our government also. This is Draco and illuminati science they do not share with the common man (their slaves and food). The Grey gave us Deep Freeze technology. They have electrodes that receive and transmit signals and can produce VISIONS and hallucinations in any human and completely control their biology.

Extraterrestrials have always had this technology. Dr. Jose Delgado while a psychologist at Yale University decades ago said physical control of many brain functions is a demonstrated fact. We can create and follow the intentions and THOUGHTS of a human, create and take away hostility, memory, sexual behavior and, emotions by remote control. The knowledge of psychic attack is standard training or programming in the illuminati mind controlled slave. The human that lacks discernment will use their FREE WILL to wait for a savior and create their own karmic debt and stuck issues to rebalance.

The universal law of PERPETUAL TRANSMUTATION of ENERGY is that all humans have the power to change the conditions in their life. Raising your vibration is hard work. You need to stay in your biology and focus your thoughts. We all have that skill set. Imbalances you attracted to you because of YOUR attachment to an agenda, thing or per- son have to be UNDONE or uncreated by you also. With all freedoms and increased awareness there are responsibilities to create win-win-win for all involved.

The GREY is the "WORKER bee" for whatever group has created and or harnessed them. The Grey comes in many varieties and does not have a soul. They don't handle the unexpected well because they CAN'T think for themselves. That is why when abductees, ask them questions they don't answer them. If an "ant," you were tormenting asked you WHY you "were doing that" what would you say to the ant?

The reptilians, Draco's, Zeta Reticuli I and II and Sirius A all have Greys working for them. Greys have been implanting generations of human family members on earth for the last 100 years and monitoring their brain waves, use greys. A select body (NSA) National Security Agency in the United States was designed to be the liaison between the Greys and earth humans. National Security Agency has became a government unto them self and is exempt from United States laws. Now some members of the NSA are considered part of "The Grey Group Mind Complex" and Communication System.

□□

ILLUMINATI creates DYSFUNCTIONAL ADULTS

Illuminist infants (close to a third of the population on earth) at 20 to 24 months old, toddlers were all trained EXACTLY the same way all around the world. There is no need to wonder WHY they are dysfunctional children and adults, sexually addicted and EMOTIONALLY arrested at around the age 2 or 3 years. You don't need a lot of education to figure out that if you traumatize, drug and electric shock an infant repeatedly throughout their childhood to "TRAIN them" you create a dysfunctional child that grows into a dysfunctional adult, parent and member of society. Our political leaders, those controlling and stealing our labor and wealth were trained like this. Those that are well known in movies, television and music stars are placed and supported or taken out by the illuminati. Most of our violent criminals are a result of illuminati programming. Most of the people trying to rid the earth of the illuminati at this time are primarily those who have defected from the "Illuminati family." Leaving them is NEVER clean or easy. It is always a struggle and possibly fatal.

The beauty of this training system is that the person has mastered dissociation to such a fine art that they re- member almost none of the training or the resulting robotic behavior. Remember the illuminati are generational Satanists. The cult does not want their members THINKING for them self. One who thinks, feels or bonds with another is harder to control and force. When an illuminati raised person starts having compassion for themselves, their programming starts to crash, their alters start to integrate, they start to heal and become useless to their handlers. Below is just a small amount of programming all toddlers get and are unable to remember if they ever get into therapy.

The STEPS of DISCIPLINE programming, comes after fetal trauma programs, Woodpecker Grid Cages and abandonment programming. Steps of discipline programming, will start at 20 to 24 months old. This programming is to train easy and fast dissociation resulting in UNCONSCIOUS loyalty to the local satanic cult or family and the worldwide network of Satanists.

1st is NOT to NEED The toddler is placed in a training room without any sensory stimulus with gray, white, or beige walls and left alone for hours or all day. If the child begs the adult to stay or screams the child is beaten and told the periods of isolation will increase until they learn to stop being WEAK. The child is often found rocking itself or hugging itself in a corner occasionally CATATONIC from fear. The trainer RESCUES the child giving food, drink and bonding. The predator becomes the SAVIOR and tells the child THE FAMILY told the trainer to rescue the child be- cause the family (the satanic cult) loves him or her.

THE ADULT and child have learned to shut down massages from their own body. They are generally not aware of THEIR own hunger, stress or the need for rest their entire life. They trust no one including them self and their own senses. They can't figure out what they did wrong, but they know it is their fault. When someone tries to help them, their response is, "I don't need any help" "I am OK" "I'd rather do it alone."

2nd is NOT to WANT Similar to the first step and gets reinforces the next few years. An adult enters the room with a large pitcher of ice water and food. If the child asks for either as the adult is eating or drinking in front of the child he or she is SEVERELY punished for being WEAK and NEEDY. The child shutting down awareness of their bodily needs is reinforced.

THE ADULT and child have learned they are not worthy of being treated in a compassionate loving way. They can understand what a low priority in the hierarchy they are. The toddler has more control over their environment than the infant does so that increases the child's options for ways to get what they want or need by stealing or telling a lie. Immediate gratification is what they strive for when there is an opportunity to binge on something, they do. Guilt over sneaking and stealing can create purging. They fear lack. In our leaders its stealing and hoarding other peoples money and services. They feel ENTITLED to verbally, physically or sexually abuse anyone.

3rd is NOT to WISH The child is placed in a room with favorite toys or objects. A KIND adult comes into the room plays with the child. They engage in fantasy play about the child's secret wishes or dreams to develop TRUST in the lonely isolated child. Later the child is severely punished for any aspect of wishing or fantasy shared with the adult and the destruction of the child's favorite toys or ANY illusion of safety the child may have left. This step is repeated often with many variations.

THE ADULT and child think the illuminati family knows all its thoughts and the fear increases. They have learned the pain will stop when they please their trainers and handlers. They feel powerless and strive to please in all areas of life instead of create and enjoy.

4th is SURVIVAL of the FITTEST starts at age 2 to create perpetrator alters in the child. ALL cult members are expected to be good perpetrators. A child, trainer and an- other child of the same age are put together. The child is severely beaten for long periods of time by the trainer and then told to hit the other child or they will be beaten further. If the child refuses it is punished severely the other child is punished too and told to punish the first child. If the child continues to refuse or cries or tries to hit the trainer instead they continue to be beaten. This is repeated until the child finally complies and beats the other child.

THE ADULT and child have learned this as NORMAL healthy

behavior and what the family wants. This reinforces the victim predator cycle that has dominated the earth the past 13 thousand years.

5th is the CODE of SILENCE As a child becomes more verbal and after a ritual or group gathering, the child is asked about what they saw or heard during the meeting. They tell what they saw and get severely beaten or TORTURED creating a new ALTER. The child is to guard the memories of what was seen on pain of death. Setups, role-playing and double binds go on endlessly to rein- force this lesson.

THE ADULT and child have learned they are always being "set up" the puzzle is they never know for what. There is no escape or anyway out. The dissociation comes so easily to them that the events in their life do not have a beginning, middle or end. There are only a lot of small pieces not connected to anything else. No flow or pattern just a bunch of abusive mysteries. It is easier to respond robotically and unconsciously. When you see them on television or in person, look in their staring eyes, with the look that "no one is home."

6th is BETRAYAL and TWINNING Starts in infancy and is formalized at ages 6-7 continuing into adulthood. Betrayal is an important dark SPIRITUAL principle. The child is placed in situations where an adult who is kindly rescues the child and gains its trust several times. After months / a year of bonding with the child, he or she will turn to the adult for help. The adult backs away MOCKING the child and abusing it.

TWINNING set ups are CREATING twin bonds in children that are NOT twins. The child is allowed to play with and become close to another child in the cult from earliest childhood. At some point early on the child is told that the other child is actually their "twin" and they were separated at birth. It is a great SECRET and do not tell. Cult children are lonely and isolated and are overjoyed to have a friend to do everything with. Later they will be FORCED to hurt each other. If one "twin" is considered expendable, its twin will kill him or her. When one twin refuses to kill, hit or hurt the other they will be brutalized by the trainer and the refusing twin will be told that the child was hurt because of their refusal to comply.

THE ADULT and child have learned not to trust their family or anyone else for that matter. Bonding and trusting is dangerous and painful. Asking for help means getting "set up" once again. You are angry and feel powerless so when they get a chance to vent or torment another, even their own children, they do.

SEXUAL ADDICTION and PERVERSIONS

Sexual addiction and perversions are trained into the infant and toddler and continuously reinforced. The children attend rituals and parties around the world to reinforce their training and be used as sexual toys or favors for the adults. They convince the child that the cult and their trainers OWN the child's body. They have no say as to what happens to them. No REAL choices are ever allowed. The Illuminati uses the ILLUSION of choice only. If you fail to make the right choice there is pain.

BETA Programming is built on Alpha programming in infants and children. The 3rd dimensional vibration or calibrations of brain waves at BETA rhythm or 12 to 30 Hz or cycles per second. At the beta vibration your reality is perceived, as "outside" of you and you feel separate and isolated. The core belief is that you are a victim or predator. BETA is the 2nd easiest brain wave to reach and is associated with aggression, survival and sexual impulses. In the illuminati the beta programming holds cult PROTECTORS, internal warriors and MILITARY systems and may be coded BLUE.

All absolutely ALL, children in the illuminati are "trained sex slaves" from birth and at 2 years are programmed to have charisma and act seductively. The adults want to believe that the child WANTS to be sexually and physically abused by them. Beta male and female alternate personalities are used as Black Widows for espionage and blackmail.

Beauty is in the eye of the beholder programmers can put almost any kind of body to use as a sex slave in the crime syndicate, pornography, movies or Internet porn. Some snuff films are of having one's head chopped off while having sex or aborting a fetus. Early sexual abuse events will be used or created to anchor this Beta programming and the alters. Beta alternate personalities generally see themselves as cats.

The SCORPION Programming was given to "Monarch sex slaves" both male and female. This frequency promotes hostility, aggression, suicide, pain, hurt and assassination. This programming is located at the root chakra and up into the reptilian brain. Sex is used as a method of survival with a great deal of trickery and deception. This vibration is frequently used in satanic rituals.

The BETA model can ONLY have sex with ones their handlers

allows them to have sex with. They CANNOT refuse sexually servicing another. Slaves are consistently belittled and compared unfavorably to others.

JEWEL and METAL Programming The child is shown a piece of jewelry or a large example of the jewel (or metal) and asked isn't this amethyst, ruby, emerald or diamond beautiful? The child will be eager to look at it and touch it. The child is told they need to EARN the right to be that jewel. So TRAINING begins with systematic abuse and trauma, drugging and electric shock to create full alters inside their programming. Amethyst is usually 1st earned and linked to KEEPING SECRETS. Ruby is next and linked to SEXUAL ABUSE and sexual alters inside. As the child is repeatedly sexually traumatized and survives they CREATE sexual alters to please adult perversions.

The level of training a child is put in is dependent on the child's parents' status or their DNA, the region he or she is born in, the group the child is born into, and the trainers that work with she or he. JEWEL programming is started at 2 or 3 years of age and is considered higher than metals to achieve it and higher levels means more abuse, drugging, hypnotism and electro shock.

Emerald generally comes at ages 12 to 15 years and is linked to family loyalty, WITCHCRAFT and dark spiritual achievement. Emeralds often have a black cat linked to them. Diamond is the highest gemstone, and not all children will earn it. "Family jewels" are often passed down internally during training sessions with trainers and family members. All high Illuminati families will have jewels hidden in secret vaults, which have been passed down for generations.

Triads of three elders may be seen in the alter system. Platinum's may have a head council of three. Jewels will have a triad of ruby, emerald, diamond in many systems, to rule over the others as an internal LEADERSHIP COUNCIL, "System Above", "Ascended Masters", "supreme council", regional council, world council, etc. may be found internally. Jewels will have a triad, made up of ruby, emerald, diamond in many systems, to rule over the others as an internal "leadership council", "System Above", "Ascended

Masters", "supreme council", regional council, world council, etc. may be found in the slaves programming. The councils found will vary with each person. It is common for the system to have internal handlers such as parents, and grandparents in their internal leadership hierarchy in a generational survivor. High priests and priestesses may sit on ruling councils inside the internal system of alternate personalities.

Any choice a child or adult may THINK they have is only an illusion of power or control of their life. To stay alive throughout this trauma based programming you must conform and perform. The easiest way to stay alive is to dissociate and do what you are told. The vast majority of these children as children or adults have no memory of the endless torment and abuse they experienced to becoming an illuminati pawn that helps control the earth. The dysfunctions and addictions they display when they are not currently in service are endless. They have surrendered their body and thought to the family (satanic cult). The ones that have become awake are taking back control of their bodies and thoughts BUT when they fall into dissociation again they become easy prey to their own programming. Being responsible for yourself, your consciousness all the time, by never dissociating, is a struggle but the only way to decide for the self your moral dilemmas.

□□

7. LIGHT, DARK and LIGHT AGAIN

As we go through the day we invest our energy good or bad, strong or weak into everything we choose to do or avoid. That activity of putting energy into other people, things or events is what makes us non-stop creators. Some create darkness as the illuminati members have done traditionally.

ILLUMINIST families are the generational bloodlines and the REAL decision makers of the secret societies that run each country in the world. An illuminati member has won every presidential election. The top of the illuminati pyramid consists of the 13 ruling families. Each family is given an area or function to fulfill like global finance, mind control, military or technology research and development, media, entertainment, news or religion. Each ruling family has a council of 13.

All 13 families are shape shifters or hybrids 50% human and 50% or more reptilian. ALL their infants are raised as Satanists with trauma based and mind control programming. The committee of 300 is the layer below the 13 ruling families in the hierarchy and supports the ruling families and follows their directives.

Within these ranks of the generational illuminati many INDIVIDUALS have moved to the light and are working with the galactic community to restructure the dark agenda and intent our masters have created for us and left us with after the TREATY of ANCHARA of 1995 ending the galactic wars with a galactic truce stating that the "dark, Anchara Alliance" and the "light, Galactic federation" all agreed to move to greater light. Some still in their biology on earth are not releasing their dark ways and choices.

The earth allies or illuminati gone light again have spent years putting together a series of temporary governments that are ready to come on line when the present monetary and economic systems fail and a radical fix will be the only way forward. The White Dragon Society members are calling for banks to work according to their Charters, and bankers who fail to comply will face the consequences of their actions. Many nations are secretly dethroning their dark leaders and implementing lighter practices and leaders.

When someone has committed and is moving toward greater light they need to release old dark ways of dealing with their setbacks, stress and upsets. When you have released an addiction and use the old methods of coping you will be going back into your old addiction or ways. When you are moving to light you need to release the old ways of FORCE, killing, terrorizing or giving them your energy by engaging in their drama to get your agenda working. Others need to join willingly. The stubborn ones must keep stewing in their own creations until they SEE the wisdom of making a different choice. The stubborn ones hurting others need to be restrained and contained. Jailed for their criminal activity and or made powerless to hurt or control others. Those under their power need to stand up and speak their truth.

After being light and aligned with universal law many humans in Atlantis decided to go dark. Then when they yearn to be light again the tools of darkness must be set aside for them to realign with the light again. In the many "round loops of events" or cycles we experience we continuously choose darkness or light and put the thought and effort into making light or dark things happen. The transition from carrying 60% light to 65% light and above can be filled with fear and magic thinking. It takes faith and strong desire to move to greater light.

PIECES, demons, remnants, bits, aspects, and alters created while you played in the dark and left behind when you moved to greater light need to be gathered up by their creator. Their energy and wisdom needs to be heard and owned by their creator. Incorporating them strengthens you the creator.

On earth all 3rd and lower 4th dimension vibrations are gone except for those still holding onto that reality. The individuals that lived in those vibrations have been relocated. BUT not all their dark energy or creations have followed them YET so a PORTAL was opened January 26, 2012 to allow the pieces, aspects, and alters to reunite with their creator in their new locations. That way family demons and entities interfering with the light illuminati members moving to greater light will have an easier time staying light and using light methods and tools restructuring the world finance policies and politics. Energy or pieces of themselves are left in all their important and sacred objects, their tools, living space, clothes, and the people they have invested their energy in.

As a creator we make aspects of ourselves to go out and experience things on our behalf. Soul is always rediscovering itself by creating aspects and identities of it self, blessing them and giving them their freedom to do as they wish. Those aspects in turn create more aspects or pieces.

When we release these aspects, they do as they wish generally. Dark creators force them to do their bidding. The way a dark parent or adult uses their child or any child they can get a hold of.

Pieces come from past lives, concurrent realities and dreams. Most commonly when we have rejected a piece of our personality, we split it off and reject it. Sometimes we send it off very wounded, and then they return to taunt their creator or enjoy sending them on wild goose chases. An aspect or piece created to handle NEGATIVE emotions or thoughts can cause major imbalances in the human. Some aspects try or DO control their creator when the piece takes on a life of its own and controls the human. You may consider it a demon when it is only an aspect that wants to be reunited with you. When you fail to embrace your pieces and aspects they can create dissociative identity disorder or schizophrenia or depression in their creator. When you feel guilty you give pieces of you away to the one you feel guilty about. Depression results from guilt and destroys your self-esteem.

Dissociation will never be helpful to you when you want to go light. The illuminati using their trauma based programming have taken splitting off pieces or alters into a fine dark art. The standard Illuminati alter system can make 2,197 alternate personalities or alters or splits in their slaves. Number 13 is considered the highest level of knowledge in the illuminati. They split off personalities for their slaves using this formula 13 x 13 x 13 = 2,197.

A soulless biology or piece of matter not guided by a soul is unconscious and frequently insensitive. When you call someone parent, friend, leader or religious advisor, check the eyes to be sure an essence with a soul is present. If they are soulless why include them in your reality. When an organism or structure is created, cloned or copied it is SOULLESS because the soul did NOT create it.

Pieces, remnants, bits or aspects made from a being with a soul are SPIRITUAL and have their creator's energy or power. You feed and sustain them. Take time to notice if you have pieces of another or they have pieces of you. All the pieces and entities need to be returned to their rightful owner or creator. Ask your soul aspect for help in locating your pieces and returning pieces, you have of others.

Now if you imagine a loved one or family member or enemy holding or hiding a piece of you that they refuse to return ask them why. Listen carefully to the answer to in- crease your awareness. Try to reason with them to get your piece back. Offer the piece of them you have. When they refuse to return your piece possibly you are flattered that they want you and you enjoy the attachment. Take an honest look at your thoughts. Attachments will hold you back.

All the bits and pieces of you that separated from you have a bit of their knowledge to share with you. Ask for it! Their information gives you many aha-moments, and helps complete and strengthen you. Know that hand-me- down values and belief's accepted under torture and duress or trauma based programming are quickly discarded. When you feel you are in a safe place your parts and pieces or alternate personalities start to integrate on their own. Integration cannot be forced and the piece or alter must trust you enough to integrate with you again.

☐☐

ADVANCED TECHNOLOGY or NOT

The dark truths have generated constant pain and suffering to point out that there is a better way to think. Very little wisdom gathering happens while living by dark truths of blame and refusal to take responsibility for your creations. Denials, lies and twisting the truth to manipulate others create more of the same. Many parents use these behaviors with their children. Darkness is not capable of unconditional love and is a caretaker at best. The history of earth with different tribes and then nations or religious groups fighting over land, wealth and the power to control others is a low technological version of what has gone on in our galaxy for the past 20 million years.

Darkness does what it always does because they are VERY wounded, angry and feel entitled to make others suffer as much or more than they feel they have suffered. Conflict or wars always start over greediness or the illusion that there is LACK in your world. When you feel powerless to create or take responsibility for your needs and wants dark steals from others.

The technologically advanced ORION GROUP felt en- titled to everyone and everything it wanted. The Orion or reptilians took what they wanted from the Lyrians by force. They claim it was a "war of beliefs" just as our wars here on earth claim to be. A group of mainly human races were committed to "service to others." The other group was a mixed group of human and reptilian races that wanted "service to self." That works well for the leaders on top that have the weaker and dependent, especially children, females and slaves to serve them. The Orion group was mainly located in the constellations of Draco and Orion.

The philosophy of service to self was very similar to communism that implied everybody takes care of them self and share equally in the bounty. That is an excellent truth in higher vibrations of unconditional self-love and ethical behavior. The dark parent or reptilian truths are that they refuse to take responsibility for what they CREATE and destroy. They are not ethical and dark's creations always wind up being one form or another of the victim / predator cycle, with lots of suffering for all especially the small and weak ones that grow up and repeat the patterns of victim- hood.

Our governments when given choices from darker alien races (law of attraction, dark earth attracted dark aliens) have always chosen advanced technology. In exchange the aliens were allowed to experiment on humanity anyway they like. The earth's leaders, governments, religions and large corporations all use humanity as a slave race and have done so for the past 13 thousand years. Our DNA is mixed with a minimum of 22 other extraterrestrial's DNA. We don't respect our self or each other on earth.

No one in the galactic community wants to baby sit the human slaves on earth, with our free will we made many dark choices. In the Galactic community we are considered immature and lacking in what it takes to survive the great shift we are experiencing. Higher vibrating aliens and extra-terrestrials don't want to be worshipped as saviors either. They want to mentor, ASSIST, not rescue us as we move into higher vibrations and universal law. On an individual basis each human is responsible for the amount of light she or he carries.

The GALACTIC FEDERATION comprises and represents over a thousand star systems in this region of our galaxy. The victims and their allies joined forces against the dark forming the Galactic Federation to protect them self from dark attackers. They are monitoring our shift and helping when they can. A rerun of what happened with Maldek, Lemuria and Atlantis is to be avoided. The federation is authorized to ensure that there will be safe places for enlightened communities to live in peace. The invisible realm has been relocating people in groups that have similar vibrations, that way it is easier for them to work with the group.

We have allowed our illuminati controlled governments to drug and dumb down our children and adults with unhealthy foods and toxic chemtrails in our skies. They prevent and suppress our awareness of the many FREE energy devices on earth. We have never gotten cur-rent scientific discoveries or accurate historical information. The secret government BLOCKS or distorts the flow of important information. We provide the labor and are the natural resource for the secret government. We have put our head in the sand and focused on personal drama, ad-dictions, satisfying the largest bully in our life and endless distractions with the unimportant material toys.

Those on earth fighting the illuminati control come from defectors of the illuminati. From the ancient secret societies dedicated to the Light that were infiltrated by the dark and turned dark. Some of the many children of the major dark families running the secret government have turned light again and are using their considerable influence and connections to turn things around. They are committed to bringing our planet into alignment with universal law. Not until the early 1990s has there been "divine dispensation" for the earth allies to focus on and carry out what needs to be done prior to a first contact with the ga-lactic society.

☐☐

PERCEPTUAL OVERLOAD is FATIGUING

Some have merged their essence with Gaia and as a result their biology restructuring causes fatigue. Some are turning off obsolete genetic codes and re-booting their DNA that has been waiting to go back on line for the past 13 thousand years that is also hard work for our biology. There is a continual increase in the planets vibration that results in change and stress on the biology. Treating your biology well and working with it is "loving yourself." Biology was not designed to do your bidding it was designed to help you experience low vibrations, separation and com- passion.

Newly activated DNA codes and higher vibrations change our perceptions and consequently our thoughts and feelings. Our senses are expanding and increasing. The biology and brain are getting downloads they do not understand or have not integrated yet. That puts our awareness into perceptual overload and great fatigue for the brain and biology that have been forced to operate in two or more different realities from 3rd to 5th dimension. As long as we have two different operating systems working in the same biology we will be fatigued.

Staying as calm and rested as possible helps. Do more of what you enjoy doing. Failing to release your past will prevent you from living in the present. We are the portals that we will open. We receive downloads through our crown or pineal gland and opened third eye. The information goes on into our opened high heart to be translated by unconditional love and compassion. Lin- ear time is getting harder and harder to stay connected with and the effort is fatiguing and disorienting at times.

Huge decisions are being made with our soul aspects and Gaia also resulting in fatigue. Linear time is giving way to LOOPS of SIMILAR EVENTS or cycles. The past, present, and future exist simultaneously as loops of similar events. The loops are not sequential. There are a large variety of possible versions of any reality. These different realities intermingle and even merge with each other. The intermingling is to help suggest or give building blocks to create new types of realities. As earth's new matrix is being decided on and created ALL other realities shift and change. Any new or different reaction by you in any loop ALTERS all the loops having those similar events. Time or "event loops" in true quantum state move in all directions. Event loops are set in a sea of potentials that constantly change. Your POINT of perception of any given event can change your thoughts.

Certain similar EVENTS or themes that we experience that may happen in any story, reality or experience. Your role or the character you play in the event changes. You may be the hero or innocent. You can be the victim, onlooker, predator or supporting one. Your perception of what is happening is colored by your role and your agenda. Are you dinning out to give YOU a treat, or make another jealous or have you made it a competition? Each dinning out experience you have gives you a window of opportunity to play a new role or set a different agenda. Are you ready to move from a competition to rewarding you and your biology? Or are you enabling another that does not want to take responsibility for the self?

You have experienced times of humiliation from one close to you. Is your reaction to feel worthless and wounded or do you have compassion for their feelings of insecurity?

There are different rules for different dimensions. In low vibrations, merging a person and vehicle might mean death. In higher vibrations the vehicle and person could experience a merging of molecules to become one and neither object gets damaged. It will be a moment of complete unity.

It is stressful and exhausting to be around darkness. Stepping away from dark ones is desirable when moving to the light. You are the creator of your reality and decide whom to associate with. When another is unable to reciprocate by giving you compassion in return for the compassion you send to them release them. When you are too attached to release darkness figure out WHY. Ask your soul aspect to help you know why. Choosing to remain in dark situations is a great temptation to forget your SELF and fall into being a wounded little human and victim. ANY person, place, situation or thing that interferes with your ability to carry light needs to be addressed, healed or released. Our greatest challenge is the thoughts WE HOLD. The problems in your life are never those around you, they are only present to illustrate what your thinking has created for you.

The light galactic society is waiting for Gaia's light quotient to be at a level that invites them to land on the surface of the earth for all to see and know. Many of the frightened and dark ones will need to log-out of this reality first. Gaia has been home to many developing societies for millions of years. Now the ascended forms of those societies are encircle her to assist her movement back into her new ascended reality. Transmutations of our biology will be synchronized with Gaia's body. The movement from our present reality into that of new earth or vibration will be barely noticed. Just a steady processes of activating our DNA that in turn changes our perceptions, thoughts and creations. Becoming master of your thoughts means you are the master of your continuing and ongoing ascensions.

The ASCENDED MASTERS or the holders of ancient wisdom or the spiritually enlightened are humans that walked the earth at one time. They aligned with universal law and their little human has surrendered to the soul and its wisdom. They come back to earth spiritually to help us. Little humans have needed to believe they were a separate individual for that was all we knew. In reality all the Ascended Masters have entered into the vibration of the GROUP MIND having one expression.

The galactic community, inner earth groups and the ascended master group are overseeing the global society's shift into a cooperative network of cultures that will be based on freedom, abundance and sovereignty of each individual aligning with universal law or moving to another location.

☐☐

8. WINDOWS of OPPORTUNITY

Time or the past, present, and future exist simultaneously so any new or different reaction you have, to your usual pattern, will ALTER all three periods of time. Your past and future is only the NOW moment in all the loops of events you have experienced in this lifetime or reality. That is why your unresolved childhood trauma or issues still affect you strongly in the now moment. The round loops of similar events or themes we all move in never go away until there is resolution. That is WHY a trauma in childhood or a concurrent life that is unresolved STILL causes you upset in the now moment. You just can't move past it until you understand what confuses you without blame or vengeance.

In the 4th dimension time is very mutable. Pure aware- ness in loops on a theme is in operation when we sleep, meditate or create because then we are thought without our biology or the duality matrix affecting us. But if you visited the 4th dimension while you slept to act out sexually, you have unresolved sexual issues you do not understand and you keep repeating your actions to get clarity. Know that you were abused because a predator existed in your reality. Know you are old enough and strong enough to protect and love the small helpless one that was you. Give that one your compassion and protection.

The law of attraction pulls similar events together and the law of entrainment holds them together for you to see and understand your thinking. Time falls back over itself like string theory running concurrently in all directions with constantly changing potentials and points of perception for you to change the direction of your life and reality.

Time is not specific like we had on earth in duality; it's an open portal or window of opportunity. The SEQUENCE of events or series of choices build on each other to create an experience with points of separation. Future, present, and past are always being recreated by each individual as their beliefs, attitudes, and associations evolve and change. When the beliefs do not change or change little you continuously recreate what you already have like boredom, suffering or victimization. Confusion about your personal beliefs creates anxiety. The linear memory of your past events is rarely what we remember them to be. So it is always wise to consult your soul aspects and get their take on events in your life. The small INNER child that has become wounded or the aspect of you that you split off from you and deny is frozen in time waiting for the compassionate adult to do something to facilitate healing and growth of the inner child or wounded aspect.

It is therapeutic for the adult to listen to what the inner child or wounded aspect has to say or share. By gathering that information, correcting wrongs and embracing the separated part you become whole. Promise to protect and comfort the traumatized inner children and pieces you split off.

Those who keep recreating the same beliefs over and over, generation after generation create the same reality with their repetitive thought patterns into "family traditions." Present time actions can and do change the past as well as the future. "Freewill" and dark choices in duality can be most painful until you gather the wisdom to make lighter choices.

Repression of negative thought doesn't work because that is really denial. Feelings of self-loathing, fear, anger, guilt, or resentment need to be looked at, recognized and owned. When your thinking changes permanently your reactions change permanently, which in turn change and influence all your realities and experiences on that event loop or theme. You will then have rewritten your point of perception in all those many experiences generally creating a more positive outcome in the now moment. See you do create your own miracles.

For example: spouse #4 is like the 3 before which treat you the same way your parent did and that is the same way you treat children. Have compassion for and protect you the small helpless one that got terrified by being pushed around by the bully. Adopt new points of perception and consequently behaviors. When you change a core belief and consequently your behavior you change the now moment PERMANENTLY. A permanent change rewrites your past and future or concurrent interactions around that issue.

For example: you have a compulsion to have the last word or be right. The law of attraction and your past experience has put you in that type of family and experiences so you have the opportunity to THINK and react differently from your past stuck pattern of opposition. The law of allowing is a peaceful way to go. Can you change your point of perception and allow others to believe what they want to believe. Tell your wounded child that you love and accept him or her just as they are. They are valuable and worthwhile to you the adult.

Be conscious of feeling the sunshine, heat, warmth and many other things. There are gamma rays, and x-rays filled with information that the sun sends. The magnetic and light energy you are exposed to impact your emotions and points of perception. New pathways and awareness are being read by your physical, emotional, mental and spiritual body then sent to the brain. Temporary blurry vision may result from solar flares that change our magnetism.

ENERGY IMPRINTS or HAUNTING is the intense EMOTIONAL interactions of humans or other entities in a particular space. A loop of information and feeling is left and played over and over again. For example in a place that there has been violent abuse, murder, a battlefield or ritual there will be a strong energy imprint left. When you are in a space or building that has held strong emotion you can feel it when you focus on it and even interface with it. The imprint or haunting carries scientific attributes that are measureable like magnetism, gravity, light, time anomalies and temperature changes on the cold side. Haunting or energy imprints are multidimensional events.

That loop of information or cycle continues to play out until there is new stronger information to make it fade away or a resolution is worked out. For example they want to be "remembered" so create some way to remember them. The imprint might want a wrong to be made right or they may need "clarity" about an event that causes them confusion.

Evil is a metaphor for the DARK a human can create with their energy. Demon possession is the work of human imbalance supported by mythology. A DEMON is an entity that is 70-100% dark. So if one of your dead relatives possesses your biology at times and they are dark they could also be called a demon. Dark entities like to help you indulge in the addictions or compulsions they enjoyed. Your awareness of them and your refusal to play their dark games make them go away. Satanic Cults have ceremonies to INVITE demons in their members especially the newborn that is trained to ALLOW demons to enter them and take over. It is real BUT always created by a human. You see what you believe and create what you focus on. Criminal acts done in the presence of light are neutralized to some degree. The light has many protectors including and especially the self.

□□

ALLOWING an ASPECT to RUN the BIOLOGY

Both Alice Miller and Freud speak about what happens when a child is asked to do too much. When children are forced to care take the adult or other children. When the child is forced to satisfy the adults needs socially, physical- ly, and emotionally and or sexually the child is asked to do more than their fair share. This puts the child's energy and their attitude way off balance. In response to unreasonable demands put on the child they may split off a large aspect of themselves to make that aspect handle the demands of the adult(s). Alice Miller and Freud say this treatment in childhood creates an adult that DOESN'T WANT TO. They don't want to do anything for anyone anymore once they have taken the power to say NO.

They are angry about their mistreatment. When they are big enough or powerful enough to say NO to most everyone and everything they do. Some like to pretend to comply and they say YES and never do it or forget about it. Some are very greedy like the small angry child they are emotionally. They want what they want when they want it. They feel it is their TURN to demand whatever they want and they want it now. Again this is the reasoning of an emotionally stunted powerless angry child.

The type of adult that has allowed an angry aspect of them self to handle their personal relationships is impossible to reason with logically. The angry aspect is a small child that was forced to do more than their fair share! Spiritually the core personality was put out of balance. To keep functioning the core personality split off an aspect to deal with the unreasonable demands. That aspect deals with problems on the emotional level it was at when it was split off. Aspects do not grow and develop they stay at the same emotional age they are at. Just as when a person starts an addiction they stay emotionally at that age. If that is a two year old they are not too logical and want what they want, when they want it. They are similar to a haunting or energy imprint that moves with the biology or an event loop or engram that operates the biology. The aspect is throwing a nonstop tantrum.

Spiritually what you are dealing with is the core personality that has allowed an "out of control" or angry or greedy aspect to run the biology. One example is the individual that functions well at work because the core personality goes to work. But at the first sign of stress in personal relationships the "out of control" or angry or greedy aspect takes over. The aspect might be whom you are dealing with at home or whom your children have to deal with.

To restore balance and harmony to the aspect you need to take the emotional charge off of the experiences and traumas the aspect had and continuously re-experiences. Ideally you would work with the core personality. But if all you have to work with is the aspect that is doable. If the human, con- trolled by the aspect is willing that is great. Most likely you will need to work with the invisible realm. Explain to the aspect that you realize that what they were asked to do as a child was way out of balance and unjust. Explain that you have compassion for all they suffered. Ask if the aspect is willing to be compassionate and nurturing to itself for all it lived through on the core personalities behalf? When the answer is yes, ask if they want to rejoin the core personality and ask the core personality if they are willing to embrace and protect the aspect. If both are in agreement then they will integrate.

The aspect may say NO to integration because the core personality has gone too dark to integrate with. We created a portal of greater light for those aspects to go through so they can reunite with a higher vibration of the soul. This is helping to clear out more of Gaia's emotional body.

☐☐

SPACECRAFT, PORTALS and PLANETS

Spacecraft, portals, planets and galaxies are sentient and intimately involved with all the entities in or on them. There is a synergy with the common purpose of support, balance and harmony. In higher vibrations there is no need for advanced technology or workers or out smarting each other or collecting a lot of stuff or power. You create for you as the need arises. Right now the light is using its superior technology and wisdom following universal law to overcome the dark ones advantages on earth. The dark ones are converting or "seeing the light" or leaving higher vibrations or they are no longer being allowed access to lighter ones and areas.

The majority of spacecraft are not machines. When we see spacecraft around the earth they look like machines that fly to match our beliefs. Just as the individuals inside the craft will appear in a form that is not too frightening to the average human. Space crafts, portals and planets can put shields around themselves that cannot be penetrated by anything we have on earth or in lower vibrations.

Generally spacecraft live and breathe and are sentient beings able to feel and perceive. Space crafts are piloted with THOUGHT. As the pilot or passengers merge their thoughts with the ship, they think or vibrate to the new location. They shrink or expand themselves as needed to match the vibration of the reality they want to be in. You merge with that frequency not GO to that frequency. This is a not so physical way to move easily between realms.

When you enter an Arcturian ship through your aware- ness the first stop is generally the Restoration Chamber to heal YOUR physical, mental and emotional ills by healing the SOURCE of those wounds. Then you allow your astral bodies to adjust to the higher frequency of the Starship or portal. Our astral bodies are 4th dimension and the Arcturian ships exist in the 5th to 8th dimension. Humans are brought on the ship when their consciousness is higher than that of what daily life on earth is.

Crewmembers also use the Restoration Chamber when they need rebalancing. The Ship is biological and communes with every visitor, it can read the thoughts and feelings of all visitors and crewmembers. The ship cares for it self and for those who visit and live within it. The space- craft feels more like a planet than a machine or spaceship.

Within our bodies, planets, spacecraft and portals the various rhythmic systems NEVER FIGHT each other they always fall into synchronized rhythms or entrainment. The principle of entrainment is universal and appears in chemistry, biology, medicine, psychology, sociology, astronomy, architecture and humans. Entrainment is the tendency for two oscillating (move back and forth at a regular speed) bodies to "lock into phase" so that they vibrate in harmony or synchronize with each other when exposed to each other for long enough. It is a synchronization of two or more rhythmic cycles. It's true of clocks and electric driers sitting in close proximity the way musicians manage to play in time together in groups.

Body systems, thinking and personalities entrain or become synchronized to their environment. Gaia and the life on and in her are currently entrained to move to greater light or higher vibration with the help of the sun and the photon belt in this quadrant of the universe. The sun is a portal of energy sending warmth and gamma rays. Earth and sun connect and stretch out through time and space by means of quanta particles passed from one to the other through solar storms. The MAGNETICS of the sun and grids are at their lowest point currently because they are being reset. Their magnetic fields are transmitting or talking to and triggering our DNA.

The "universal law of ENTRAINMENT" requires two vibrations existing in the same space MUST adjust and combine to have a single resonance. A mathematical example to explain entrainment is using a number line with zero at the center and positive numbers on one side and negative numbers on the other side of the number line. A darkness of negative 3 would need at least a + 3 to neutralize the darkness or REMIND the dark that it comes from the light. Dark can return to the light if it chooses to align with universal law but it will take more than + 3 in change of thought and behavior. Another example, on a scale of 1-10 if one person is at 2 and the other is at 8 they are required to both be at 5ish with the law of entrainment. Or when one person is overpowering it will pull the other to their level so both would move to 2, or 3ish or to 7, or 8ish. "The PRINCIPLE of Reconciliation" allows different qualities to become unified to diminish differences and decrease conflict and promote similarities and harmony in all things sharing the same space.

Examine your relationships and notice how in sync you are with the seen and unseen in your existence. Entrained is having your energetic field overlap another's energy field so that two or more of you can get in sync to support or create a common purpose. This law goes into effect when you share space within a portal, space- craft or planet. Entrainment can be noticed in your event loops of the past and future. At a crime scene or battlefield or rally or celebration you feel things from the others that shared that space from another event loop. Know that who or what you share space with AFFECTS YOU or you affect them to enhance or focus on your commonalities.

When you worship or revere dead relatives or ancestors you are entrained with them and their energy. How light were they? How were they victims or predators and is that energy supporting you to be a victim or out of control? Consider what you do and the energy you are currently en- trained with. When your energies mix with anyone the law of entrainment or synchronicity kicks in. Do you like and approve of the energies you share with others?

The law of attraction and entrainment work with each other and compliment each other. The attraction "brings it" and the entrainment helps to "maintain it without conflict." When you stay entrained with the energy of a per- son "with or without" biology, a job, house, area or country much darker than you that helps you stay darker. That is your choice and the law of attraction will keep bring more of what you have settled in with. You can choose to with- draw your energy from the entrainment and end it because without energy the entrainment falls apart. But no one will or can do it for you.

Ideally you are entrained with your invisible soul aspects. If you have brought them to a lower darker vibration, now is the time to bring you first, to a higher vibration and they will follow you to greater light. Just as they followed you to greater darkness to support and help you while allowing you to have free will and experiences with dark truths.

□□

KNOWING you VISITED with ALIENS

To know you have done a thing, your beliefs need to embrace the possibility that you could of done it. The good things in life can't be touched generally but we do feel and have awareness of them, because we believe in them. We believe in and feel things like love, acceptance and transference of energy and feelings. Human's essence can and does; bi and tri locate. Your biology is not needed for your essence or awareness to be in a different location or loop of events. If the little human rejects the concept that part of your awareness was hanging out with an alien but that happened, you will go into confusion and consequently denial or forgetfulness. Especially when you say to yourself but I was watching the movie the entire time. I couldn't of been also "kicking it will" Hal the alien from Orion.

Humans need to be able to accept that there is life on other planets far more advanced technologically and spiritually than earth is. Just as on earth there are darker nastier humans there are dark planets too. Both the dark and light entities on other planets happen to be more advanced technologically than entities on earth are. Other realities do not have linear time in their illusion and they function in the now moment all the time. In present time there can be many encounters that happen all in the same moment. Our essence and awareness can be spread very thin.

We have mistakenly thought about dimensions as being sequential and or separate. Dimensions have different THEMES or purposes with different vibrations that all interact with each other. They can move and shift as easily as our thoughts do. Dimensions travel in circles the way light travels in circles. Many meetings with other entities are not really PHYSICAL meetings. Humans can blink into higher dimensions and not realize that happened. Human essences' can ask questions, give information, receive information or attend a lecture, class or discussion or just hang out.

Trying to squeeze what really happened—your aware- ness took a class in a higher "not tangible dimension"— into your belief, "that if it didn't happen on the physical plane," it can't be. Meetings happen all the time in slightly higher frequencies than the physical plane. A long meeting can appear to be a short period of physical time. Our knowledge of these encounters are not erased, we are just not consciously aware, but they are stored in our aura or the bodies that surround the biology. The human brain vibrates too low to read the memory accurately because it needs to be strained through your beliefs. After your rather limited beliefs interpret your experience, you go into con- fusion that may create anxiety or depression in you. When you can reassure the brain it is not in danger and it might just be having new and interesting experiences the anxiety or depression will leave. Instead of thinking new and different information is dangerous try enjoying the adventure of it all.

The third dimension has been so difficult for humans that adding awareness of another reality seems to be an overwhelming task. Higher vibrating realities are much more enjoyable to experience. To BE in higher vibrations you need to match their frequency. You need to vibrate at the same rate the reality you want to be in, vibrates. In reality, you do not "go" to another reality. You merge with that frequency. YES, that goes against all the rules of our physical world but that physical world is leaving for many of us. To vibrate higher you need to focus your intention by surrendering or falling into the feeling of that experience and vibration. Unconditional love is abundant in higher vibrations and holds all the realities together.

Higher dimensions can view or are aware of all the lower dimensions. The galactic community, living in higher dimensions than we do, has communicated with us for all of our existence. Higher dimensions do not use words and languages to communicate with. They accept information into their knowingness that surrounds them. Humans with low self-worth and doubt have trouble accepting telepathy or pictures or thought transference. Telepathy is the ability to receive others' thoughts weather the person sending them knows they were transmitted or not. Transference of thought is when both beings are aware of what each other are thinking. The invisible realm has endless meetings with our essence to create a consensus. There needs to always be general agreements for everything that goes on in our experiences. However humans frequently do not remember that an agreement or consensus was arrived at. Questions were asked and discussed about having certain experiences and agreements were made. Experiences are totally dependent on the intention and desire of the individual and or group.

We have had a very long experience with darkness and suffering and are over ready to return to higher vibrations. We move to higher vibrations as we CLEAR our own personal darkness and fear. Then there is mastering the law of allowing and compassion for the self. Leaving duality and the illusion of time allows us to remember every- thing we have ever experienced in all our now moment. The little human beliefs are that we cannot live in two or more realities simultaneously. These are the lower frequency emotions of 3rd dimension. Our awareness has almost expanded enough to perceive 5th dimension compassion and sensory awareness. There is grieving about leaving the reality we have learned to live in and function in. Many of us are over ready to return fulltime to unconditional love and compassion.

This ascension is HUMAN ASCENSION when the individual chooses it.

This ascension is a GALACTIC and PLANETARY ascension that is in process. There are always many perceptions of the same event. The individuals on and in the earth can be divided into three different groups. One group is moving to the 5th dimension, beyond the fear of change and into unity and unconditional love. The second group stays in 4th dimension until they are emotionally aligned closer to universal law. And there are those choosing to experience more drama and battle between light and dark to free themselves from opposites and "I am better than you" or "I have more stuff than you do."

☐ ☐

9. PLANETS are HALLOW

All planets, suns and moons created naturally are hollow in the middle. In Life magazine November 10, 1967 is a photograph of earth taken by the lunar orbiter showing a 1,600-mile diameter passage into earth at the North Pole. Earth is hollow with openings at the poles.

VENUS used to be a moon of Uranus. MERCURY was a moon of Saturn. There are nine artificial moons in our solar system.

The reptilians refurbish moons and planetoids and create their own internal ecosystem and fit them with propulsion. They use a gel for fuel. An asteroid dragged our moon across the galaxy to our solar system, more than 11,000 years ago. The same asteroid circles our galaxy every 25,156 years. The Draco's used the moon as a space- craft to go from Draco to earth. Our MOON is older than the earth and has been inhabited off and on for the past 1.8 million years. There are entrances at the poles of the moon. Taurus mountains and the Jules Verne crater and Archimedes were all entrances on the moon when the Orion Group had our moon.

Moon soil is 6.2 billion years old and has compounds and chemicals not found on Earth. Lunar soil did not come from the rock that makes up its mountains and craters. Many of the original structures on the surface of the moon were destroyed during wars fought by humanoids against the Orion Empire. It has ruins, monuments and bridges all over it. Many of the craters on the moon were used as spacecraft hangars. Larger craters housed 200 or more craft. Some craters are 170 miles wide. The moon has pyramids that act as balancing weights like the ones we put on fans to keep them spinning smoothly.

The hidden dark side of the moon has many large living spaces and irrigation underground. Humans and reptilians live inside and on top of the moon. It has an atmosphere similar to earth in many places.

Our MOON is a satellite with bases on and "in" it and is colonized with Americans, Russians, British and French, personnel and many hybrids. The Greys took the humans to the moon sometimes by force. Some of the greatest scientific minds, engineers, and architects have vanished and taken to the moon or Mars. There is a full time working population of 35,000 people. The military complex is underground.

A select body (NSA) National Security Agency in the United States was designed to be the liaison between the Greys and earth humans and became a government unto them self. Exempt from the United States laws. Some members of the NSA are part of "The Grey Group Mind Complex" and Communication System. BLACK MONKS are from the National Security Agency and have been on the moon since the 50s. Earth's moon is a jumping off point to colonize Mars.

The BLUE MOON unit in the NSA has bases, alien technology and information on the moon. Blue Moon on earth is underneath Kirkland Air Force base in New Mexico. The entrance to this base is in Manzano Mountain and the private Department of Energy (DOE) techno- logical base. The building of free energy devices for use in space is ongoing. Under Blue Moon there is a group called Alpha One and they gather materials and make sure the population doesn't know much. Alpha Two deals with personnel and seeing that their belief system is in harmony with dark.

MALDEK was the 4th planet in our solar system. Our present Moon was one of two moons that orbited Maldek. Maldekians were a mix of Lyrians and Reptilian. The Reptilian population was smaller and controlled by the Lyrians. The souls that were leaders from Maldek became our global banking families like the Rothschild extended family is. They continue being reborn into the same genetic family to retain their control. These illuminati and Russian elite are consciously aware of their Maldekian incarnations. Currently they are replaying the same nuclear scenario on earth in hopes of changing the outcome. Most are UNDER the United States living in underground illuminati cities and facilities.

Million years ago, the Orion group (illuminati) united and built up dark forces on the planet Maldek to attack our solar system and others. In response to the Orion terrorism and to prevent more attacks on a Pleiadian planet the Galactic Federation planned a counterattack. They arranged for a "battle planet" to come into the solar system and destroy the planet Maldek and consequently the Orion Group base of operation. An atomic explosion destroyed colonies on Earth, Mars and Venus. The chain reaction destroyed billions of lives and reduced the planet to rubble of various sizes that orbit the asteroid belt in its former orbit between Mars and Jupiter.

NIBIRU or MARDUK or BATTLE PLANET X or 12th planet from the sun is a reptilian built, mechanized world orbiting our solar system. It has a 3,600 year orbit and is coming close to earth in 2013-17. This planet is enclosed in a shell that generates its own heat and is 2 and 1/2 times larger than earth. It was an off world headquarters of the dark or Anunnaki since the time of Atlantis.

ANUNNAKI or ABBENNAKKI or NIBIRUIANS live on the mechanized world and before that they came from Draco. Females from Orion and male's from Sirius B mated and the off spring of a new Reptilian race was created and named "Nibiru" and a tribe became a race. Between visitations to earth the Abbennakki employ small beings they call "Bear" to monitor earth.

SATURN is the sixth planet from the Sun and the second largest planet in our Solar System, after Jupiter. Saturn is classified as a "gas giant" having an average radius 9 times larger than Earth's with only one-eighth the average density of Earth. The interior of Saturn is probably composed of a core of iron, nickel, silicon and oxygen compounds, surrounded by a deep layer of metallic hydrogen, an intermediate layer of liquid hydrogen and liquid helium, and an outer gaseous layer. The metallic-hydrogen layer gives Saturn's planetary magnetic field, which is slightly weaker than Earth's. Saturn has nine rings and sixty-two moons.

In Egyptian mythology Isis is considered Saturn's eldest daughter. "El" is the god Saturn and supreme deity represented as a black cube. Masonic authors clearly associate Saturn with Satan and the lower nature of man or the little human and its limitations, restrictions, death and decay. The "grim reaper" originates from the god Saturn holding the sickle that he killed his father with. As said in Star Trek, Saturn gives off a gas Reptilians "get high" on.

PLANETS are SENTIENT

Planets are not static they are sentient and have life cycles. We are experiencing transformation and changes in environment with Gaia at this time. She needs to reinvigorate herself and Gaia is doing that now just as she has done many times before. The difference now is that all the life forms and humans chose to stay on the planet this time. Generally they are taken off planet during this part of the renewal cycle.

Along with all the water changes come weather changes. The amount of water on earth dictates the various TEMPERATURES and winds found on earth. The water cycles control the winds and the temperatures. The ice on earth is melting at the poles and is a natural occurrence. As the ice melts, cold water moves into the oceans making them raise a few inches and cool some creating larger storms than we are accustom to. The ice melts from underneath and has nothing to do with pollutants in the air. When the ice melts there is a huge shift in weight on earth. The weight of the water is redistributed on the earth's crust. Where the earth is thinner or weaker you get earthquakes and volcanoes. The most powerful earthquakes will hap- pen closest to the poles. There are unique places on Earth where the crust is thinner and spongy. The ocean floor beneath the gulf coast is soft and brittle like crackled glass. The oil in that region is leaking from more than one place and seeping into other waterways.

The water temperature cooling the oceans starts or triggers the renewal process. A cold period always starts with warming from underneath to melt the ice and is what some have called global warming. In these water cycles there are large ice ages lasting 400-years, small cycles lasting 150-year ice ages and medium size water cycles like the one we are starting now. The last small ice age was in the 1200s to 1400s. Right now we are starting a medium water cycle or ice age. During the renewal process we will lose some species and gain new ones that is a normal part of the renewal process.

The earth is 71% water. Gaia and everyone on earth need fresh water to maintain health refresh and renew our self. That is why humans dream of water or rain or rivers. Water moves, rests and brings energies back into alignment. Water on other planets does NOT have the liquid WET that we have. Dirt or ground on earth isn't found on other planets either. Over

78% of the fresh water in the world is in North America.

97% of water on earth is Saltwater because the reptilians or illuminati put salt into our oceans to make them un-drinkable and create a LACK of fresh water. That way they can charge for and distribute a natural resource we cannot live without. When you control the fresh water you control the food and the people that cannot exist without fresh water.

A planet and those that live on and in the planet are impossible to separate, they balance each other.

The GALACTIC ALIGNMENT is the alignment of the December solstice sun with the Galactic equator as a result of the precession of the equinoxes. Precession is caused by the earth wobbling very slowly on its axis and shifts the position of the equinoxes and solstices one degree every 71.5 years. This Galactic Alignment occurs only once every 26,000 years. The energy of the Galactic Alignment is a 36-year window ending 2030 and 2012 is the midpoint.

On December 21, 2012 Earth will be directly in front of the Galactic Center and the transformative energies will be streaming directly into our personal and planetary body. It is so close now that increasingly intense energies are already creating rapid changes in our world. People are CHOOSING what they want to create. By 2030 we will see the start of real peace on earth in the Middle East. The teenagers now will be the leaders then with new potentials, solutions and new technology.

The high frequency light coming in from the Galactic Center and into our planetary consciousness brings a new way of perceiving reality. Instead of fear being our first re-action with change we will be more open and accepting as we are getting increasing amounts of unconditional love.

Gaia's heart chakra or the Kundalini, is seeking an-other center of wisdom or balance. The masculine energy of strength and aggression does not honor the land, air, or water. The southern hemisphere of earth carries a more feminine energy. Those from the north that wanted to conquer or enslave caused wars fought in the southern hemisphere. The northern hemisphere of earth has more masculine energy. Most of the major wars and all of the world wars were started and fought in the north most of the time. The portals of more balanced softer wisdom or di-vine feminine are the energy of Machu Picchu, a sweet safe energy. The wisdom has always been there to be placed on the Crystalline Grid of the planet and shared with all but not accessed.

The crystalline grid responds to human awareness or the Kundalini of earth. This energy moves or uncoils itself ONLY when called to do so by our awareness. The planet being out of balance affects the grids. Now that humans are changing and becoming integrated and more balanced so are the grids. The magnetic grid, the crystalline grid and Gaia's consciousness are all invisible grids inter- twined together. All of these energies are catalysts to each other.

The GALACTIC GRID or COSMIC LATTICE is the energy field around earth and includes all the grid systems and magnetic patterns we have on, in and around the earth. The lattice holds the current illusion together, which is in transition now. It is an omnipotent source of energy not measurable with our current technology. All the grids are formatted to allow all within them to expand creatively. The cosmic pulse within spiral galaxies forms a creation pattern spiral that lends it self to physical matter and duality.

Each galaxy has a collective consciousness or the living energy field that is the sum of its entire species. The universal mind is awake and aware.

2010 the Milky Way populations broke down into 70% human, 25% reptilian and 5% others.

2012 it is 79% human, 14% reptilian and 8% others.

☐☐

CLEARING GAIA'S EMOTIONAL Body

GAIA is the SOUL or consciousness of earth and a living, sentient, breathing being able to converse with all life on earth and in the universe. She is the human's support system emotionally, physically and spiritually. For the past 13 thousand years there has been a grid of dark around earth and the universal law of attraction brought more low vibrating entities to her and us. The lower 4th dimension was (it is gone now) the place 80% of us went to after we lost our biology. We carried a rather small amount of light with or without our biology. Similar in theory to "Dante's Inferno" Hell is depicted as nine circles of suffering or the universal law of attraction brings the same type of offenders and victims together.

The groups brought together in the lower 4th dimension would be the lost gray soul aspects clinging to addictions, compulsions, blaming and forcing others. Humans visited Mystery Schools for spiritual training and enlightenment on each sub plane of the 4th dimension during dreams or nightmares and meditations. They visited the "cities" in the lower astral plane of endless illusions and distortions. The entities or ghosts are filled with despair, hopelessness and blame. They create endless dramas and wars to generate fear and psychic energy feeding in the lower 4th dimension and with the ones still in biology. Lower astral beings are psychic vampires, possess humans with less than 70% light and encourage humans to hate them self. These entities are frequently your relatives, dark aspects of you or illuminati trainers and handlers. The lower 4th and 3rd dimension was their playground.

These "repetitious patterns" of behavior we get stuck in feel like eternal punishment and damnation. When you consider yourself bad, evil or unlovable your choices in life and after death are very limited. A channeled individual from the lower 4th dimension does NOT know more than they did when they were alive in the 3rd dimension. They will misdirect you in the same ways they did when they had biology or were alive. Discernment is always needed.

Guidance, healing and wisdom are the same thing. Your future is YOUR balanced, healed energy of your past. To move to higher vibrations you need to want to heal the self as NO ONE can rescue you or do it for you. Anyone that says they are here to "save" you is telling dark truths. When we ask others for healing or guidance our emotional body automatically opens up to the healer or possible outside manipulation. Messages and healing from higher dimensions or vibrations come as a flash of light or awareness or pictures without negativity. The dark soul aspect needs to start thinking outside the box to heal. Too often they took another biology and lifetime to relieve their suffering with- out gathering any new spiritual awareness.

Historically Gaia has released her pockets of dense energy with extreme weather like earthquakes and volcanoes. Since humans are ascending for the first time with their planet she asked for help clearing out the darkness from her emotional body. When dark entities or pockets of density are released into "a portal of greater light" they are not around to possess and torment the living and Gaia can carry more light. A portal of greater light is the point of separation from the dark near realms INTO higher truths and feelings. It is common for our dead parents to show up for more awareness and help from their children. When they have the awareness they then need, please help them get to greater light. Moving to greater light and awareness increases their and your vibration.

Several friends of mine have easy communication with the invisible realm and in 2004, I was asked to increase the awareness and understanding of those lost in the circles of suffering and trapped in their victimhood of having been sexually abused. For an hour or two each day for a few weeks I would read or talk aloud about sexual abuse to those that would listen, without their biology. This creates a loop that keeps playing in the invisible realm to any new comers that wanted to access the information. I talked of how devastating child sexual abuse is and how negatively it impacts a person of any age. The sexual abuser does what was done to them. By repeating this behavior (compulsion to repeat) of forcing another in the same way they were forced, hopefully they will remember what happened to them and have COMPASSION for when they were being victimized. Compassion for self when you were victimized heals the trauma so you can move past that wound and go to greater light. Then we invited all the sexually abused to move through the portal of greater light and out of the lower 4th dimension. There were millions that went to greater light and more awareness. Gaia's emotional body got lighter and so did the earth.

The darker ones need someone lighter to help him or her "go to the light" or "cross over" or go to the "bridge of flowers" because dark repels light. Any human can take souls directly to greater light so they do not get side tracked or lost in the near realms. Ask the soul if they are ready to cross first, respect the "no." Invite any other souls around to move to a portal opening of greater light you create in your mind or encircle your arms for them to enter and move through.

Then I taught about sexual predators. That they are individuals that have no compassion for the little abused child they were. They feel justified in hurting others to avoid FEELING their own pain. Then there were angry abused females and males that wanted JUSTICE and revenge they had righteous indignation. They could not move past their pain and suffering, someone needed to pay! They were unable to embrace the fact that they attracted those experiences to gain spiritual wisdom. They failed to have compassion for the victimized child they were and FEEL their pain. They failed to remember the ones they perpetrated on and their suffering.

There are those waiting to be rescued by a god or leader. They bought into the belief that "another can do it for you" or rescue you. I needed to explain that they needed to follow their own internal wisdom and be there own hero. That is the way of it. There was a large group waiting to be LOVED by an external source, parent or god. They had to learn to love themselves first.

The next group was the retarded, emotionally disoriented and children that were institutionalized. They were confused and disoriented. First they needed comforting and calming and we directed them to a portal of greater light to get rest and clarity. There were aborted fetuses with souls that we helped move to more light.

Others came to the portal of greater light that were not taught first. They included aliens, planets and stars. Various individuals and those around them came also.

On July 29, 2011 we educated a legion of dark (illuminati good old boys) about how destructive their abusive parenting was to their children, spouses and grandchildren handing down those dark family practices. Once again you did what was done to you. The way to heal it is to have COMPASSION for the abused child you were with no one there to save or understand you. To take responsibility for comforting and protecting the small infant and child they were. We are here to experience not blame or punish. No one blames you or wants to punish you. Comfort and protect the small child you were. Are you ready to move to greater light and comfort?

August 7, 2011 we worked with Gaia to remove more pockets of density on the earth, moon and Mars. We brought a portal of greater light to move dark and dense areas into it to transmute them to higher vibrations. We started collecting density from different countries and bodies of water and life in the sea and on earth. We sent the scars of wars, violence, abuse, atomic and nuclear weapons and fault lines on earth to a portal of greater light. We put a portal of light around the "illuminati force field" around earth to control and isolate us. It is being transmuted now.

We brought a portal of light into the hollow earth at both poles to release darkness in Agartha as 15% of the Agarthans are darker than light and working with the reptilians. In the crust of Gaia the illuminati have bunkers or cities and they are hiding out from the surface of earth that they have scarred and poisoned to kill many of us off with toxic food and chemtrails. By August 11, 2011 Gaia had 87% light. With more light there can be LESS extreme weather.

Gaia wanted the people on earth to ascend with her. 13 thousand years ago she asked for volunteers to experience the darkness we just pasted through. Those that could survive that would become strong enough to participate in a planetary ascension with her. To ascend you must release the emotional charge from your dark experiences. We are here to heal all the dark experiences the human family created for itself to increase its spiritual wisdom.

We are no longer separate individuals that blame. As children blamed parents humans PROJECT their shortcomings onto their soul when they fail to own what they have created with the many little dark choices the little human made daily. Blaming your soul will block YOUR communication with your higher self and invisible aspects. Blaming others will keep you stuck. There are no others to point the finger at in the 5th dimension. Any movement made by one individual in the group, all experience.

The template we created as humans to help Gaia release the dark in her emotional body was given to other planets to use.

The core of our Milky Way Galaxy is aligning and merging with the Andromeda Galaxy at this time.

☐☐

10. LEADERLESS MOVEMENT into LIGHT

The movement to light is leaderless because inside you know what is right. All you need to do is act on it all the time. Consider that dark and light use all the same universal laws and principles. When you operate in the light "give and receive only compassion" by treating others as equals, being transparent and being compassionate with you, harmony and balance are easy to maintain and enjoy. Especially if those around you are also doing what they know is right for them.

When individuals in your reality or our leaders put a DARK SPIN on the universal law with their deception, force, greediness and self-hate it's hard to discern the universal law in action when it gets so twisted and dark. Personal discernment is critical to avoid those using dark truths. What is happening now is a leaderless revolution. As individuals have compassion for them self and stand for who and what they are, others "observe that" and gather strength from your strength. The support helps them have compassion for the self and they want to stand up for fairness and equality for them self. Following a leader any leader goes against "give and receive only compassion" because following another means you have also given them the BURDEN of being responsible for YOU. Your thought, your feelings and your direction, being the leader or follower is a dark truth. We all have the innate sense of what is right or light within us. You only need to listen and act accordingly.

Whether your behavior is DARK or LIGHT the law of attraction brings us more of what we have already created in our reality. When we are in alignment with universal law we enjoy more of the same. If you are not enjoying what you have created for you, then you are not listening to your self and acting accordingly. You get more of what you choose, to POINT out to you, the thoughts you operate with that are not so compassionate to you. When you want to go lighter you need to be aware of WHAT your thoughts are. That is how you will know which thoughts to redirect.

The dark ones AGENDA in your life is always to control YOUR goods and services to benefit them. Even when they say it is for "your own good" and they love you. These are LIES to manipulate with. Criminals, dark aliens, dark spouses and parents and dysfunctional families do that to each other generation after generation. Just as dark leaders, political and religious do that to their followers. They take care of each other or give fake love and attention only as a "set up" for you to be used once again. That is "fearing the bully" or "being the bully" game. Time to stop playing that dark victim predator cycle and OWN that you created the reality you have with your very own thoughts or dissociation from thinking.

To help and support us moving to lighter thought, our soul aspects are setting up ENTRAINMENTS or SYN- CHRONICITIES for the little human. This is frequently one human in your environment helping another human. But it isn't always with a human; it could be with an animal, rock, tree or event. That is how those following universal law support each other not by being a leader or follower. The OTHER that supports your increased awareness can be anyone you are creating with.

An example of entrainment in the classroom is put- ting two students together working on the same subject and one understands a bit more than the other student. The one seeing the bigger picture helps the other to understand how it all works together. One student learned a new concept and one mastered the concept with greater depth and understanding. Both students felt compassion- ate towards each other. They gave and received only compassion without judgment, force or agenda.

Another example is a landscaper hired to create beauty and order in a yard that reflected the chaos in the owner's emotional body. The owner had asked his soul for help. Soul aspects of each person met and agreed to lining up this synchronicity to last for around 3 weeks. The landscaper and homeowner's emotional body were over- laid so they each sensed the other's emotional body for those weeks. The one with the chaos would be supported to create order in their emotions if they chose that. In the process of entrainment with light you are supportive and hold a space for the other to get different perceptions or awareness of their yard and emotional reactions.

Our biology gets dysfunctional to get our attention when we are not being compassionate with it. Biology is not something to force or control. It operates like a space- ship if the essence and the biology are not in balance and harmony you aren't going anyplace. If you need to find an expert to support you in healing yourself, your auras will overlap to ENTRAIN your resonance and their resonance or vibration for a period of time. The stronger vibration SUPPORTS the weaker more limited one and gives an example of the larger picture to consider and to expand truths and options. Your invisible soul aspects line up the synchronicities to share informational energy. This is creating the opportunity to make lighter choices within free will. That is freedom.

The earth, sun and photon belt are entrained with overlapping auras to bring greater light to this quadrant of the galaxy. May 1998 the earth entrained with the pho- ton belt and the first of its twelve gigantic homogenizing vortexes of light HIGHLY magnetically charged. These frequencies are to rebalance all that enter. It takes 2,000 years to pass through all the vortexes. In 2001 Gaia, many humans, cetaceans, animals, plants and the mineral kingdom moved to the 4th dimension. Photons can raise and expand our levels of awareness by shifting our perspective to a higher vibration and the much larger picture. When you vibrate at 80% light or more you can control photons in the now moment. We can entrain with them to accomplish tasks with our compassion and clarity of thought.

Waves of light from the sun, sun flares or gamma rays are being released at various intervals and are particularly strong during the EQUINOX and SOLSTICES. As years pass the light released intensifies to create even deeper spiritual cleansing to leave lower vibrating realities. GAMMA RAYS are electromagnetic radiation of shorter and higher frequency wavelength than X-rays. Gamma rays serve as harmonizing frequencies that store our perceptions of what we see, like an object's size, color, texture, function, etc. Gamma brainwaves are thought to be associated with brain function that creates holographic synthesis of data stored in various areas of the brain to fuse them together into a higher perspective.

The more imbalanced or darker we are, the more disruption and internal conflict we will feel during entrainment to greater light. Those of us from Atlantis that made dark choices during that event loop are having an opportunity to choose compassion this time.

During this process of moving to greater light, SEPARATION between the dimensions becomes thinner or goes away completely. Photons are gathering on and around earth circulating in the air and collecting and being stored in water. By 2030 photon energy will become the predominant energy and will change the magnetic field on earth so much that no existing technology will work then. Our cars, radios, televisions, planes and computers won't work after the great shift because photons will REPLACE electricity. Photons are a form of infinite electromagnetic energy found on the subatomic level and the basic unit of light and all other forms of electromagnetic radiation.

Photons gather thoughts, have memory, think, evolve, do NOT have a past or future and are self-directing to any need that is present in the now moment. Photons can transfer energy from one end of the universe to the other end and not be diminished as they travel in a vacuum at the speed of light and have both wave and particle proper- ties. Photons carry electromagnetic radiation of all wave- lengths like gamma rays, X-rays, ultraviolet light, visible light, infrared light, microwaves, and radio waves.

We are in an ENTRAINED GROUP AWARENESS of a leaderless movement. The individual chooses the speed and direction they want to align with GIVE and receive only COMPASSION.

☐☐

HOARDING is a WOUNDED HUMAN

SELF LOVE in those that carry more dark than light is twisted into greediness or lack. The universal principle of COMPENSATION is that we receive "like energy" to the energy we emanate in our thought and action. The universal principle of LIABILITY says we are held liable for the use, abuse or neglect of the rights we have and have earned.

Humans, countries and planets that are being fiscally irresponsible are crying out to be nurtured and loved. They are wrapping themselves in material things or forcing animals or others to care for their emotional needs and that never does it! Any nurturing or compassion you have been denied needs to be given to you by you.

SELF LOVE in those that carry more light than dark is nurturing and caring for the biology and soul or spirit. That needs to be mastered by you and for you before you TAINT others with YOUR neediness. Limitation or lack comes from your refusal to see, own and use the wisdom or clues offered to you. Synchronicities, "gods gifts" or the legion of lights blessings need to be allowed in or received by YOU. The one that can and does nurture you is you and your soul together. No one or thing can do it for you.

The universal principle of PROSPERITY is you pros- per in direct proportion to the enjoyment you receive in seeing the prosperity of yourself and others. Your prosper- ity is denied in direct proportion to your feelings of guilt, envy or hostility for being prosperous or witnessing other's prosperity. When one prospers all may prosper. Maintain a prosperous attitude even in states of poverty to move to prosperous states.

ALLOWING is the higher vibrating way to love the self first. Allow the dark ones their choices without your judgment, upset or interference. Do not give the dark ANY of your energy. When you include a dark one, in anyway into your ISSUE or life you get wounded or disappointed with the result. Stop trying to rescue another from the choices they made, ALLOW. When you insist on including the dark, selfish and chaotic one OWN that is YOUR neediness and desire to FORCE another. You are being dark and creating more darkness for you because you are demanding the dark change. THEY are not your problem. You are your problem.

You need to stay light FIRST. Stay light following only your soul or inner truth and you. Every time you include dark ones you CREATE a WOUNDING to yourself and you go darker.

The hoarder of any kind has given up on loving them self and "sucks the life or energy out of what they hoard." Siphoning energy from ANY external source never satisfies. Just like killing someone to get what he or she has never gives it to you. You get as good as you give. The hoarder has put them self in a state of poverty by DEMANDING some- one or something needs to love or care about them or they dissociate wallowing in their wound. The only way out is for them to CHOOSE to nurture and have compassion for the self.

The universal principle of POVERTY is that you are "in poverty" to the degree you withhold your productivity or energy in hope that someone else will offer his or her energy instead. You have unfairly claimed the energies or love or life force of another and squandered it by forcing others to do what you have not done for yourself.

Poverty comes to those fixated on penny pinching or collecting excesses of trash or hoarding animals because such a narrow focus is imbalanced and creates lost friends, poor health and lost opportunities. Focus on ONE thing at any cost is imbalance and very dark.

Poverty comes to you when you are productive and FAIL to properly take hold of your reward (energy) in a suitable manner. This is self-sacrifice and not at all spiritual. Those convinced that they are unworthy or incapable of having anything of value will be in poverty as again, self- love is lacking. Joy and wealth come from WITHIN you and never externally.

February 27, 2012 a portal of energy was opened to support humans in their love, acceptance and nurturing of the self.

The foundation that dark built and operated with is in its death throes and crumbling. Just as the behaviors we thought would protect us in the dark illusion tie and bind us to that crumbling illusion. The belief that suffering and sacrifice are good is dark truth and an easy way to control you.

Earth has emanated darkness a very long time and statistically your relatives and ancestors would be dark and YOU have been or are a dark ancestor and relative. We choose our parents based on their beliefs that MATCH our beliefs and the beliefs of the community they live in. The law of attraction brought the three of you together and the 3 of you entrained your energy way before your conception. We telepathically connect to our entire family or birth situation and the community we are born into. The infant can be overwhelmed by the situation they chose to learn a spiritual lesson in and die as an infant. Or their biology may keep living but "fail to thrive" or retardation sets in or they become chronically depressed, oppositional or dissociated. The infant is aware of the self-hate, blame and anger the family carries and generally will adopt those feelings also.

The human soul aspect may be entrained with other family members or made a contract to rescue a parent or sibling and that is the dark vibration of rescuing or care- taking. The law of allowing is not in place. Then when the child fails to rescue the parent or make them happy the child feels guilty and worthless increasing self-hate. Broad- en your perceptions and awaken to all the lies and deceptions we have accepted as truth just as our ancestors have.

REFUSING to have compassion for you first, creates SPIRITUAL DEBT for you to rebalance.

☐☐

ENTERING / LEAVING DARK EXPERIENCES

We are all aliens that came to earth. Eight million years ago a species of land cetaceans resided on earth and were the guardians of Gaia. When their civilization was destroyed some left and others took to the seas to become the whales and dolphins of today. The cetaceans asked for guardians of the land. A two-million-year search came up with aquatic primates nearing full awareness. The original human colonists on earth or the Lemurians came from the planet Vega in the Lyra constellation. They or we agreed to take on the responsibility of sustaining the earth and creating a society that honors and sustains all individuals.

Nearly a million years ago near the end of Atlantis our many little dark, greedy, controlling choices slowed our vibration and Gaia's. We devolved into dark truths and limited compassion for the self. Humans and Gaia have emanated cloudy, confused, darkness for the past 13 thousand years and we were spiritually quarantined. Earth was ravaged by the dark Anchara Alliance and we played along joining the victim predator cycle of feeding off each other and self-hate.

Freewill and darkness are only found in lower vibrations, planets or dimensions. Illusions are only found in the 3rd and lower 4th dimension. Free will means the human gets to choose when, how, why and where they want to experience their lessons. WHAT spiritual wisdom you need to gather is decided on before your birth or incarnation on earth. You must transfer a soul aspect into a human biology to be in the earth illusion, that is one of the games rules. An- other rule is that when you incarnate into biology your

DNA carries the magnetic characteristics of the collective. Individual DNA reflects the amount of spiritual wisdom or light the planet has at the time of its birth or when a soul transfer happens. Most of us were born when Gaia carried 41% light or less. We kept reincarnating hundreds of times into darkness.

By divine intervention and with the help of many, many aliens, Gaia, many humans, cetaceans, animals, plants and the mineral kingdom moved to the 4th dimension in 2001. In March 2011 the lower 4th dimension stopped existing because Gaia's vibration was higher than the lower 4th dimension. By November 2012 Gaia, plants animals and some humans will be vibrating in the 5th dimension. No more reincarnating into darkness. Historically groups and religions have gone dark on earth, they are not generally a good way to go lighter.

The collective spiritual essence of a community, nation, or ethnic group is the "group soul" and provides guidance and focus for the group. When the group or planet gets imbalanced it creates its own karma like those from Atlantis, Jewish, Mormon, Catholic and Nazi groups have done on earth. The group soul is created with the birth of the group, it strengthens and weakens to reflect the direction of the group and dies when the group disbands or merges with another group. The group from Atlantis that made so many little dark choices are here in biology again to have an opportunity to change their moral choices individually. New opportunities arise for us continuously to make lighter choices.

The process of going darker generally starts with individuals within the group that have dark or negative purpose. They have an agenda of covert force to control the services and or goods the group and individuals create. Group members go along with the dark agendas because they didn't discern the lies or deceptions they are told, they refuse the responsibility to think for the self or they enjoy the perks the dark gives. The light ones that think for them self leave the group to allow the dark their path. New dark ones are attracted to the group and join. The group gets darker and darker because dark feeds off and uses each other. The lighter ones leave.

During any civilization that evolved faster than the rest of earth civilizations there was a group incarnation of volunteers that wanted to increase knowledge, hope and lighter choices. During the golden ages of the Roman Empire, Egypt and Greece the volunteer soul group, challenged the political, economic and or religious dogma of the day. The volunteers were subjected to the same dark pressures and fears of living on earth the rest of us need to deal with daily. Many got darker and darker like Mosses and his followers. Many of the Indigo, Crystal and Rainbow soul groups of children raised in violence and trauma have gone dark. The lighter soul group has an edge. They vibrate higher and stay in communication with their soul aspects that give them support and information when they ask for it. They must ask because this is a planet of free will.

The Indigo children arrive en masse in the middle 1970s to middle 1990s. Crystal infants from 1980s to 2000, Rainbows 1990s thru 2010 and there are some Integrated children. Each soul group of children is increasingly lighter than the group before. Indigo children had gathered their spiritual wisdom on earth. Crystal children came from other planets vibrating higher than earth and had a rough time adjusting to our darkness, lack of self-love, guilt and fear. Crystal, Rainbow and the integrated child are from other planets like Sirius, Pleiades or the whales, dolphins and elementals. "The children shall lead them" in learning self-love and self-worth.

The new soul groups of children read others thoughts and are confused by our self-doubt and need for please others. They generally have unconditional compassion for the self that we misread as arrogance. Dealing with the darkness found in their families, religions and governments is a challenge for them. Because they are accustomed to manifesting whatever they want completing tasks in this slow vibration is hard.

Then there are those of us that have been reincarnating forever on earth learning spirituality the hard way immersed in darkness. As we rise in vibration we become the ICRs special light operatives that are incorporating all the various jobs of the new soul groups and integrating them to close this cycle of education and experience with dark truths. The higher frequencies of light historically have always been beyond our perception.

Round time is SEQUENCES of events having moral choices to make along the way. An experience can hap- pen in the past, present or future as they are connected together as a feedback loop. The same types of experience or events are grouped together. For example grouped together are the same moral choices found at the end of Atlantis, the end of the Roman Empire and the end of duality on earth. When you change your behavior pattern to more light in anyone of these event loops all the others change too. It doesn't matter WHEN you decided to change something in a particular loop of similar events because the dark thoughts and behaviors keep being recreated in different ways until you choose lighter choices. When they do not change or change very little you continuously recreate what you already have. The law of attraction and entrainment hold it all together for you. Feelings of self-loathing, fear, anger, guilt, or resentment are negative emotions that need recognition by you. Own your feelings so YOU can change them. Restructuring your beliefs to align with universal law will release negativity. Choosing must be followed by acting to see your chosen reality manifest.

□□

11. FEELING WHEN the dark ones SIPHON

In the 3rd dimension we operated with the "dark rules of survival" and staying alive. We have been raised on, taught, were used and controlled by dark truths. Religions and darkness do not want people to love themselves. They want a compliant worker that does not think. To continue surviving the darker ones have always siphoned light energy from lighter ones. Frequently that is a dark parent or adult siphoning energy from their child or spouse. Considering you do live on earth you can assume you have willingly or unconsciously allowed others to siphon the life out of you.

Higher vibration higher truths and allowing siphoning or feeding the dark ones with your light needs to end enabling is a dark truth. You need to keep your light energy for YOUR use. We create at the LEVEL of LIGHT we have and are able to keep. You are as light as what your repeated thoughts are. When you care take (control), allow or think about one or many dark ones your light is being siphoned by them. That means you are not showing compassion for you or them. In reality you are feeding the dark and trying to manipulate the dark ones. That makes you darker. Not being able to stand someone opens you up to being siphoned. You are giving them EXACTLY what they want— your energy.

The universal law of ACTION means the human must ACT first to start their thoughts moving in another direction. Make the many little moves in thought that prove your commitment to a different direction. Then your soul aspects will line up synchronicities in the vibration or level of compassion you function in.

The universal principle of COMPENSATION is that we receive "like energy" to the energy we emanate in our thought and action.

The universal principle of LIABILITY says we are held liable for the use, abuse or neglect of the rights we have and have earned.

The law of the triangle or trinity of consciousness at the universal level is to hold and radiate the QUALITIES of divine light, WISDOM, and the will of the legion of light. Give and receive only compassion. This says NOTHING about feeding the dark ones to keep them alive.

The higher vibrations from the sun and photons on earth are waking us up and making us feel. When we feel we think about how we feel. Maybe you want to change something you feel. Decide and choose again over and over again. Ask your soul aspect to help you FEEL when and WHERE and how large the tube is on your body the darker one is siphoning from. That way you can mentally cut the siphoning tube or cord stealing your light energy. Withdrawing your energy from a dark one makes them seek a more willing target. When your soul alerts you to your energy being siphoned you will have awareness of exactly how OFTEN and CONTINUOUSLY you are feeding the dark ones.

Emotions and entrainments move one step at a time up or down. For example when you are entrained at hopelessness emotionally you can move up a notch to depression. OR if you are at depression you can move down to hopeless. From depression you can move UP to "feeling relief from depression" and on up to revenge, hopefully only in your thoughts. Then you might move UP to anger because you are feeling stronger and having a sense of injustice about feeding dark ones frequently for many lifetimes and all it did was keep them strong and dark, while depleting you. From anger you move UP to pain and your pain body. Many living in pastime keep bringing their pain into present time. From pain you move up emotionally to vibrate at antagonism. Anger and antagonism can also give you more clarity and control of your thoughts and emotions. As your vibration changes the law of attraction will bring you different types of experiences.

Manifesting or creating starts with your awareness, curiosity, desire or intention and is the "smallest unit of energy." Then the law of attraction brings sub atomic particles and photons that line up with your curiosity, desire or intention to start the building process. You can also create by deciding what energy is to be REMOVED. We can create and destruct in all directions of time and space. When you want to rid yourself of a dark one take away your energy or focus on them and do not allow siphoning. Cut tubes or cords as soon as they are attached to you. Any drama or upset you have, any need of yours to prove you are RIGHT or that you are the smartest one OPENS YOU up to be siphoned. You trying to control another with guilt or sarcasm or condescension OPENS you up to be feed on.

Full awareness of the now moment is knowing, sensing, feeling, hearing and seeing all that goes on around you. That is the skill to be mastered just as it has always been. Focusing in on what you want to focus on. With higher vibrations comes so much more of everything. With 60% light and higher we are able to start loving and having compassion for our self. At 70% light entities can't take over our biology and possess it. OUR consciousness is what determines our   DESTINY not the technology we operate.

When you are in perfect balance there isn't aging or disease or worry about survival. No need for emotional drama, hoarding or death that we created in the lower vibrations to feed from.

A few of our soul aspects have FOLLOWED the little human into dark behavior and lower vibrations going against universal law to maintain contact with their human aspect. This may have started many life times ago and they got stuck repeating the same dysfunctional patterns as the human did. Soul contracts were made with other dark souls that many people are STILL honoring today. There have been MANY dark lifetimes of codependency or being in the victim / predator cycle. Our darker soul aspects have helped the little human honor these "dark soul contracts" set up with other dark humans and soul aspects long ago or even recently. The human needs to take the lead to change or evolved out of any dark patterns and break the entrainments by their actions and saying "No more" out loud.

Lack of personal and spiritual growth depletes energy that is why the dark siphon the light ones. We build our individual vibration with every thought we think, emotion we feel, and belief we hold on to. Your emotion or vibration negative or not isn't judged it simply reflects with CLARITY what is in your energy field. Seeing the larger picture enables you to release past rage and current angers or frustrations. The darker spaces in our life helped us grow.

□□

You NEED to CUT FEEDING CORDS

FEEDING or VAMPIRISM or SIPHONING energy from others is what low vibrating entities do to each other. They feed off of each other's fear and negative emotions. Your negativity or fear or anger feeds the one tormenting you or creating drama or fear. You and a family member may be feeding from each other. When you hate them and they torment you that is feeding. When you sabotage an- other because they are not nice to you are feeding each other some pretty dark energy. When you feel you are better than another or entitled to make fun of them or humiliate them, dark feeding is happening.

Alcohol consumption to excess alerts dark entities you are available to be fed on because you feel sorry for yourself. Drugs work on other levels, impacting the 3rd eye and crown chakra mostly. That leaves you open for feeding because you are not in control of your biology. Those without biology feed on you also and you feed them with your self-hate and dysfunctional behavior.

Feeding cords are electromagnetic strings of energy. These cords are visible to the invisible realm and some humans see or feel them. The cords are used as feeding tubes to everything and everyone you have an attachment to. There are cords to and from beliefs, events and others we have known in this lifetime or concurrent life times or other dark realities. There are cords to those you verbally assault and are cruel to. Drama always creates cords or siphoning and feeding. Low vibrating parents siphon large amounts of energy from their children through cords of fear or control and sexual addiction. Cords can come, from or to, the biology or any of our etheric bodies. Even after physical death cords can be fully functional.

The SIZE of the cord shows you the depth of YOUR or their attachment. The location of the cord on the body speaks volumes about your relationships with that person, event or place you are sharing a cord with. Energy of all kinds, black, white and all the shades of gray energy going back and forth from you and to you from what or who is at the other end of your cord. You may be supplying light energy and they may be sending you black or dark gray energy to transmute.

Cords help you stay connected or keep you entrained in an emotion or thought pattern of energy. Like I hate her or I love him that served you in the past. It was important to our survival to know whom we could trust or not trust. Hanging on to your OLD beliefs and entrainments, ties up some pretty intense dark energy like fear, anger, betrayal, guilt or a shared belief. When you start going lighter and the other person goes darker it is time to cut cords. Old spiritual masters could be entrained with up to 1,000 people. Moses was entrained with the Jews from Egypt and he started turning dark at the end of that lifetime. Higher vibrations carry no cords they have sharing, detachment, friendship, compassion and constructive purpose. Your fondness for the Roman Empire or Egyptian lifetime may have energy cords and siphoning going on. Attachments hold you in duality and low vibrations from other lifetimes.

It matters not how you decide to cut cords. Mental- ly get out a tool or two like scissors, a chainsaw, sword or what ever turns you on. I use a round blade that circles me and I move it from my head on down and swing a blade at the top and bottom to cut all and any cords. You may have to cut cords many times to get your point across or convince your self connection with dark ones is not helpful or constructive for you. When you withdraw your energy from any dark relationship and keep the cords cut it will end. BUT if you keep dragging the dark one back into your life for ANY REASON things will probably stay as they are. The two of you will keep the gray feeding going.

HOLDING THERE LIGHT or SERVICE to OTHERS

Many spiritual writers say things like the plant, animal, elementals and mineral kingdoms volunteered to come to earth to help humans "hold their light" or you will hear that Sam holds light for Kelly. That is the "pretty story" or higher vibration way of saying that lighter groups and individuals are allowing darker groups or individuals to siphon their light. That way the darker one FEELS LOVED and fed or nurtured (care taking). As a planet, individual humans and sentient beings we are releasing the dark truth of feeding from each other to survive and moving to the higher truth of each holding our own light or loving the self.

Compassion for YOU needs to be first. Then the compassion you give others is pure. When you don't care for you first what you give is tainted with your neediness, darkness, negativity or unconsciousness. Our beliefs dictate our behavior and feelings. As long as you believe you are here on earth to SERVE the needs of another you will create more of what you have already experienced.

Caretaking and service to others first has been glamorized

especially by religions to keep us in line and working hard for the top of the pyramid or our needy parent(s), spouse or boss. Caretaking, enabling and service to others first is a way to blackmail others into valuing you because you have been taught NOT to value yourself. When you sacrifice for another that is very tainted and poisonous to the one you gift your sacrifice too.

The more you serve, care take or force the less freedom the other has to be what they want to be and the less freedom YOU have to love yourself. Wisdom and allowing are mastered individually. Allowing is unconditional love for you first and allowing others to do as they wish first. Allowing is the knowledge that everything is as it ought to be. Service to others first and then you is against universal law.

☐☐

SHADOW PEOPLE or the GRAY SOUL

Without your biology you are your soul essence. Your essence reflects the amount of light you the individual, carry based on your alignment with universal law. The soul essences on Gaia are various shades of gray. Not human law or planetary law but, give and receive only compassion. The shade of gray or ratio of dark to light you carry influences your judgment, your perceptions and the reality you have created for you. Darkness or dark gray limits the choices you perceive as available for you. The amount of light you carry triggers the law of attraction and entrainment to bring you more of what you have already created for you. This is clearly reflected in the reality you created, experience and live in.

BLACK is a 100% unbalanced and means your thoughts, beliefs and behavior patterns are totally out of alignment with universal law and you are on the way to being recycled. You are not giving or receiving compassion.

DARK GRAY or very unbalanced means you are operating with very dark truths and not morally ethical. You deny culpability for your thoughts and actions. You emanate and attract and reflect darkness. You can still turn it around to lighter if you want to.

DARK or UNBALANCED means your thoughts and beliefs have a dark bias and you are not to be trusted. Your practice of following or fearing others translates into worshipping a false god or idol instead of having compassion for YOU first. Dark choices and the illusion of power can be very seductive, addictive and intoxicating for the little human unaware of the infinite essence in the finite biology. When we continually choose to blame, force, control, humiliate and glorify being a victim, our soul aspects or higher self follows the little human into grayness to keep up the connection.

The largest areas of seduction are SEXUAL and / OR the belief that another human can KNOW more than you and your invisible aspects or soul conglomerate know. When you decide to follow another because you fear them or think they have greater spiritual wisdom or trickery that is not higher-level truth. When the soul has followed the human's lead into darkness it is a challenge to find your way back.

LIGHT or BALANCED you are caring for your essence and biology first so you emanate pure light. The human is a shade of gray when the ratio of dark to light is not a 100% dark or light. Your soul aspects will refer to people as dark or dark gray and they are cautioning you that the person is not ethical, honest or trustworthy; they are dangerous to play with and should not engage with them or counted on. Deception and twisting the facts is a dark truth.

When you desire to align your thought and behavior with universal law you are working on ascension and the little by little process of alignment. Ascension is a measure or scale of the step-by-step process of getting in alignment with universal law. That is why your essence, aura, DNA or astral body can appear shadowy like; it reflects the amount of light you carry.

Generally we can't see a shadow person but if you do see or feel one you may know them or not. If it was a person that controlled or manipulated you in life they might still be trying to control you without their biology when you allow that. Physical death doesn't keep the dark away. Your fear keeps your vibration low enough for them to siphon your energy, just as they have done you are engaging with them.

Many spirits or essences just drop by to say Hi! There are spirits that do not realize they are dead or have unfinished business or are so attached to controlling their STUFF or controlling others and blaming others they won't cross over or go to the light until they have what they feel is justice or what they THINK they are owed.

Eighty percent of those that died would get lost in the fourth dimension or the gray world and their spiritual wisdom would stay at a standstill. They were locked in THEIR dark patterns of behavior. VICTIM,

PREDATOR and CONFUSED INNOCENT thought patterns, all three states of consciousness, reside in the same slow low resonance and carry the same lack of compassion for the self and each other.

Humanity tends to pull out ONE action or ONE cause or ONE effect and treat it like it is the entire story. Totally disregarding the chain of events that created that particular state of consciousness. A chain of events that may well of started in another reality, lifetime or dimension the human doesn't remember. But what they are doing in this lifetime WILL reflect the SAME thought patterns, they are continuously repeating NOW, without resolving them, without adding compassion for the self and others. They continue to blame, judge, punish or withhold to AVOID responsibility and moral culpability for not being compassionate.

Made in the USA
Las Vegas, NV
30 November 2021